TECHNIQUES FOR BEHAVIOR CHANGE

FOURTH PRINTING

Techniques For Behavior Change

APPLICATIONS OF ADLERIAN THEORY

Compiled and Edited by

ARTHUR G. NIKELLY, Ph.D.
Clinical Psychologist
Associate Professor of Health Science
University of Illinois Health Center
Urbana, Illinois

Foreword by

Alexandra Adler, M.D.

Medical Director
Alfred Adler Mental Hygiene Clinic
Clinical Professor of Psychiatry
New York University School of Medicine
New York, New York

Epilogue by

Rudolf Dreikurs, M.D.

Director
Alfred Adler Institute of Chicago
Professor Emeritus of Psychiatry
Chicago Medical School
Chicago, Illinois

CHARLES C THOMAS · PUBLISHER
Springfield · Illinois · U.S.A.

Published and Distributed Throughout the World by

CHARLES C THOMAS · PUBLISHER

BANNERSTONE HOUSE

301-327 East Lawrence Avenue, Springfield, Illinois, U.S.A.

ISBN 0-398-01401-9

Library of Congress Catalog Card Number: 75–128649

First Printing, 1971
Second Printing, 1972
Third Printing, 1976
Fourth Printing, 1979

With THOMAS BOOKS *careful attention is given to all details of manufacturing and design. It is the Publisher's desire to present books that are satisfactory as to their physical qualities and artistic possibilities and appropriate for their particular use.* THOMAS BOOKS *will be true to those laws of quality that assure a good name and good will.*

Printed in the United States of America
00-2

CONTRIBUTORS

ALEXANDRA ADLER, M.D., Medical Director, Alfred Adler Mental Hygiene Clinic; Clinical Professor of Psychiatry, New York University School of Medicine, New York City.

JOHN A. BOSTROM, M.D., Staff Psychiatrist, Associate Professor of Health Science, University of Illinois Health Center at Urbana.

PAUL BRODSKY, M.A., Certified Psychologist, Instructor, University of California at Los Angeles.

MABELLE H. BROOKS, M.A., Counselor, Educator and Social Worker, retired; St. Petersburg, Florida.

RAYMOND J. CORSINI, PH.D., Psychologist in private practice, Honolulu, Hawaii.

EDITH A. DEWEY, B.S., Counselor and Educator; Don Mills, Canada.

DON DINKMEYER, PH.D., Professor of Guidance and Counseling, School of Education, DePaul University, Chicago, Illinois.

RUDOLF DREIKURS, M.D., Director, Alfred Adler Institute of Chicago; Professor Emeritus of Psychiatry, Chicago Medical School, Chicago, Illinois.

EDWARD A. DREYFUS, PH.D., Associate Director, Student Counseling Services, University of California at Los Angeles.

BERTRAM P. KARON, PH.D., Professor of Psychology, Michigan State University at East Lansing.

DAVID LASKOWITZ, PH.D., Director, Drug Abuse Section, Lincoln Hospital, Department of Psychiatry, Bronx, New York.

RAYMOND N. LOWE, ED.D., Professor of Counseling Psychology, University of Oregon at Eugene.

HAROLD H. MOSAK, PH.D., Clinical Psychologist in private practice, Chicago, Illinois.

O. HOBART MOWRER, PH.D., Research Professor of Psychology, University of Illinois at Urbana.

ARTHUR G. NIKELLY, PH.D., Clinical Psychologist, Associate Professor of Health Science, University of Illinois Health Center at Urbana.

WALTER E. O'CONNELL, PH.D., Research Psychologist, V.A. Hospital, Houston; Lecturer, University of St. Thomas, Houston, Texas.

GENEVIEVE PAINTER, ED.D., Director, Family Education Association of Champaign County, Champaign, Illinois.

ERNST PAPANEK, ED.D., Professor of Education, Queens College, City University of New York at Flushing.

FLOY C. PEPPER, M.S., Coordinator of Instruction, Multnomah County Intermediate Education District, Edgefield Lodge School, Troutdale, Oregon.

MIRIAM L. PEW, M.S.W., Social Worker and Program Assistant, Amherst H. Wilder Foundation, St. Paul, Minnesota.

WILMER L. PEW, M.D., Psychiatrist, Amherst H. Wilder Child Guidance Clinic, St. Paul, Minnesota; President, American Society of Adlerian Psychology; Dean, Alfred Adler Institute of Minnesota.

LEO RATTNER, PH.D., Certified Psychologist, Director of Center for Psychotherapy, Forest Hills, New York.

BINA ROSENBERG, M.D., Psychiatrist in private practice, Chicago, Illinois.

BERNARD H. SHULMAN, M.D., Assistant Professor of Psychiatry, Northwestern University Medical School, Evanston, Illinois.

VICKI SOLTZ, R.N., Consultant, University of West Virginia, College of Human Resources; Faculty of the Alfred Adler Institute of Minnesota, St. Paul.

ESTHER P. SPITZER, M.A., Psychotherapist, Alfred Adler Institute, New York City.

ADALINE STARR, M.A., Consultant, Illinois State Department of Mental Health; Psychodramatist, Alfred Adler Institute, Chicago, Illinois.

DON VERGER, ED.D., Head, Department of Psychology, Wisconsin State University at Platteville.

To My Parents

FOREWORD

Techniques for Behavior Change is a valuable addition to the publications commemorating the hundredth anniversary of the birth of Alfred Adler. It points up the basic soundness and the vitality of the principles he developed in his lectures and writings throughout his life.

Adler was born in Vienna, on February 7, 1870, and received his medical degree from the University of Vienna. From his earliest student days, he was interested in problems of mental health and illness. In 1907 he wrote his book on organ inferiority and its psychologic compensation, in which he first described the impact of inferiority feelings on the structure of the personality. His later writings developed the important concepts of the goal-directedness of the neurotic symptom, the unity of the personality, the life style, the interpretation of dreams and early recollections, the significance of the ordinal position of siblings, and finally, the concept of social interest as a measure of the individual's relation to his world.

The psychotherapist will find help for his work in this book. He will see how the relation between therapist and client can be a constructive human encounter, in which the client learns to compensate for what he has missed in his earlier life. He will be shown how the client, through persistent encouragement, learns to make the right use of environmental and biological complications, rather than being controlled by them. Sibling rivalry and other family problems are discussed in considerable detail.

Alfred Adler always encouraged his students to keep in close touch with developments in the world around them. The authors who have contributed to this volume have done so, in particular when writing on student rebellion, drug addiction, and delinquency, some of the most pressing problems facing society today. The papers which comprise this book, written by experienced psychotherapists, and compiled and edited by Arthur G. Nikelly, represent a lasting tribute to the work of Alfred Adler.

ALEXANDRA ADLER, M.D.

ix

PREFACE

DIRECTED TO PRACTITIONERS in the mental health and education professions as a modern guide to the essentials of psychotherapeutic technique, this volume aims to initiate and stimulate interest in practical approaches for modifying or retarding deviant and pathological behavior. Treatment techniques which are less speculative and more easily applied and which can be utilized not only by mental health workers but by professionals within the related correctional, preventive, and educational disciplines are the particular emphasis of this book.

This book does not attempt to introduce a new theory of psychotherapy but presents in simple terms and a straightforward manner methods by which the psychotherapist can induce change in behavior through a consideration of the facts surrounding the client's life and his direct, conscious, observable experience as presented to the therapist. Together with explaining basic therapeutic operational procedures applicable to various manifestations of maladjusted behavior, the book suggests what type of action the therapist should take in specific situations and what type he should avoid. Because this volume is intended to serve as a useful source for the training of professional workers, there is less emphasis on diagnostic labels and greater stress on the assessment of observable behavior, on the dynamics of interaction, and on methods of inducing behavioral change.

The present cultural emphasis on material values and the relative impersonality and anonymity of our society make imperative the development of methods of therapy which stress the uniqueness of each individual and his capacity to help himself. Rather than concentrating on uncovering childhood traumata, past injustices, or "unconscious" motivations in order to explain current problems, the approach described in this volume focuses on the client's present behavior and presents therapeutic and preventive methods which mobilize his feelings of responsibility, cooperation, conscientiousness, involvement, self-respect, and creativity. The therapist draws upon the client's ability to choose realistically and to make commitments, thereby strengthening his interpersonal relations and enabling him to cultivate a sensible outlook on life by taking into account the current demands of reality. Such a view of psychotherapy is based on an optimistic belief in man's amenability to change.

The techniques for behavior change described here are based upon the assumptions that human actions are forward-oriented and self-directed, that each person, based on his own values, self-concepts, and consistent style of perceiving and responding to his environment, has an innate capacity for developing an emotional and social connectedness toward those with whom he interacts. Only when these factors are taken into account will behavior change be most effective. Maladjustment, then, is not viewed as a "disease" but as a faulty adaptation to life due to personal misconceptions, mistaken goals, misconceived beliefs, distorted experiences, inaccurate conclusions, and decreased anticipatory thoughts. These inappropriate adaptations can be eradicated or modified through reeducative procedures which bring about a cognitive reevaluation within the individual and lead to a corrective experience and a desired change in behavior.

The purpose of this book, then, is to provide in a clear and systematic form a refined, operational, and reality-oriented approach for the management and treatment of maladjustment in persons of all ages. It is hoped that this volume will broaden the perspectives of psychological understanding and technique by equipping the therapist with more experiences and by giving him sufficient skills to understand the individual's condition and produce a desirable change in his behavior.

These practical techniques have emerged from the teaching and writing of the Viennese psychiatrist Alfred Adler who was born exactly one hundred years ago. Hence, this book is a tribute to him for his invaluable contributions toward the understanding and treatment of human maladjustment. The therapist will not become an expert on Adlerian techniques merely by reading this book but, hopefully, will enrich his skills and acquire an optimistic perspective in the treatment of maladjustment.

A. N.

CONTENTS

PART I

INTRODUCTION TO THEORY AND PRACTICE

PART II

ASSESSMENT TECHNIQUES

Contents

PART III

BASIC THERAPEUTIC TECHNIQUES

PART IV

GROUP TECHNIQUES

ACKNOWLEDGMENTS

I WISH TO ACKNOWLEDGE my indebtedness to Dr. Raymond J. Corsini for persuading me to undertake the preparation of this volume and for his many constructive and stimulating ideas.

I am especially grateful to Dr. Rowena R. Ansbacher and Dr. Heinz L. Ansbacher for providing me with an enormous amount of editorial advice and for their many useful suggestions regarding the content and organization of this volume. Their continued interest and support in the editing of this book has been invaluable.

Credit is also due to Dr. Bernard H. Shulman for his careful and critical reading of several chapters of the manuscript and for his suggestions for significant revisions.

Gratitude is similarly expressed to Cathy Bohstedt, Audrey Hodgins, and Don Masterson for their assistance in improving the manuscript by organizing and expressing several of the main ideas more clearly and to Alecia Shutovich, Terese Follett, and Sue Crawford for aiding me in the typing of the manuscript.

Most importantly and most obviously, I owe my indebtedness to my generous collaborators without whose contributions this volume would not have been possible. Finally, although they are too numerous to name, I wish to acknowledge those colleagues who have profoundly influenced my outlook toward those who are troubled, who have taught me to be optimistic and human, and who continue to inspire me.

A. N.

TECHNIQUES
FOR
BEHAVIOR
CHANGE

Ταράσσει τοὺς ἀνθρώπους οὐ τὰ πράγματα, ἀλλὰ τὰ περὶ
τῶν πραγμάτων δόγματα . . . ὅταν οὖν ἐμποδιζώμεθα ἢ ταρασσώμεθα
ἢ λυπώμεθα, μηδέποτε ἄλλον αἰτιώμεθα, ἀλλὰ . . . τὰ ἑαυτῶν
δόγματα. ἀπαιδεύτου ἔργον τὸ ἄλλοις ἐγκαλεῖν, ἐϑ' οἷς αὐτὸς
πράσσει κακῶς. ἠργμένου παιδεύεσθαι τὸ ἑαυτῷ. πεπαιδευμένου
τὸ μήτε ἄλλῳ μήτε ἑαυτῷ.

It is not things themselves that disturb men but their
ideas about things . . . When we meet with troubles, become
anxious or depressed, let us never blame anyone but . . . our
opinions about things. The uneducated person blames others
when he does badly; the person whose education has begun
blames himself; the already educated person blames neither
another nor himself.

———Epictetus, *Encheiridion*

Part I   Introduction
To
Theory
And
Practice

1

ADLER'S BASIC CONCEPTS: NEUROTIC AMBITION AND SOCIAL INTEREST

O. Hobart Mowrer

THE TWO CONCEPTS in Adler's writings which seem to have the greatest power and generality and which are the most meaningful to me personally are those cited in the title of this chapter. In a recent article entitled "New Directions in the Understanding and Management of Depression," [6] I have written at some length on the many penetrating implications which these two concepts have in the field of psychopathology; and here I can do no better than to select certain highlights from that article to emphasize the importance of Adler's profound and prophetic understanding of the pathogenic nature of much personal ambition and the healing power of social interest. I should like to begin by quoting an especially clear and penetrating passage from Adler's book, *The Problem of Neurosis*, published in 1929.[2] Here Adler says:

> The neurotic is paying the price of taking the most difficult, lonely, and impracticable way to the summit of his ambitions, when there are much easier and better paths. In a sense it may be said that the prototype never relinquishes its rule over the individual's life, but there are better and better ways of fulfilling its law.
>
> We must regard the love-problem as the most intimate and organically-determined form of the problem of social behaviour, a view which acts as a continual corrective of mistakes. This view of Individual Psychology may not bless us with an absolute truth; it may not enable us to foresee the future of a marriage as accurately as we can

5

calculate the path of a falling stone. But the stone lies in a world of truth, whereas we live in the realm of human mistakes. Our method enables us to replace the great mistakes by small ones, and that is our justification for believing that we can often help others to approach their own goals with a method which, if perhaps not infallible, is better than theirs in a social direction. In the world of the psyche there is no principle of individual orientation beyond our own beliefs. Very great are the consequences of our real beliefs. *Big mistakes can produce neuroses but little mistakes a nearly normal person* (p. 62) [italics added].

When this passage was recently brought to the attention of a psychiatrist friend of mine, who is not formally an Adlerian but whose views and practices are in many ways parallel to those of Adler, he exclaimed: "Excellent! That says it all, as far as my general psychiatric theory is concerned." There is, I am sure, a far wider appreciation of this point of view today than there was two or three decades ago, when Freudian concepts were in the ascendancy.

That the views presented in the foregoing quotations are in no way singular but instead reflect the tenor of Adler's entire professional career and life work is indicated by the following passages quoted from Adler by the Ansbachers.[1]

> In a neurosis we are always confronted with a highly placed goal of personal superiority. When applying the principles of Individual Psychology to the investigation of such a case, this goal of superiority can always be demonstrated as permeating all phases of life and all attitudes of an individual to his problems, from his earliest childhood on. For therapeutic purposes, this has to be shown to the individual carefully and kindly. That such a highly placed goal of personal superiority betokens a lack of the proper measure of social interest and precludes the development of a healthy interest in others is understandable. *The striving for personal superiority and the nondevelopment of social interest are both mistakes. However, they are not two mistakes which the individual has made; they are one and the same mistake* [italics added].
>
> . . . We always find that in cases of neurosis we are dealing with comparatively less active individuals who naturally, by virtue of the unchanging or unchanged style of life, were even in their childhood characterized by the lack of activity required and desirable for the correct solution of their problems . . .
>
> Neurosis is the natural, logical development of an individual who is comparatively inactive, filled with a personal, egocentric striving

for superiority, and is therefore retarded in the development of his social interest, as we find regularly among the more passive pampered styles of life.

What happens, however, to children who manifest the pampered style of life, but seek their chances of success in a more active way? They, too, do not look upon others as fellow-beings. They, too, live under the pressure of a conception of the world in which they expect to receive everything from others, or in which owing to their greater activity, they take everything from them. But the comparatively more active children are much less in danger of becoming neurotics. At a given moment, always dependent upon an exogenous factor, that is, a difficult situation, they tend to become criminals (pp. 240–241).

In view of their great psychological cost, neuroses and psychoses may be described as nervous breakdowns. The extent of the breakdown is appraised by the extent to which the patient is prevented from normal participation in society, its demands and its benefits. It is the exclusive and isolated individuals, whose contact with life has always been loose because of their exaggerated personal ambition, who will resort to such abnormal distance from the demands of society. These are the neurotically disposed individuals. They are characterized by a false attitude toward all life problems, the social, the vocational, the sexual problem. The false attitude consists in regarding these demands as merely personal, private affairs and overlooking the common relationship and general implications.

This is the reason why in the face of threatening or actual defeat such people will easily lose courage. The amount of threat a person can bear without losing courage may be called psychological tolerance. *Psychological tolerance depends on the strength of social ties.* If the tolerance is exceeded, this will in turn reflect itself in the attitude toward the demands of life. "One cannot ask so much of me; one must take my disorder into account." "What couldn't I accomplish if I were well." Everyone has something of such an attitude. The psychological tolerance is undermined by failures, some of which are certainly to be expected. Encouragement can strengthen the tolerance and prevent, ease, or defer the outbreak of a neurosis (p. 243) [italics added].

Warner and his associates,[10] in their sociological study of a New England community, which they called *Yankee City*, report the observation that there is an unusually high incidence of emotional instability and suicide in ambitious, successful, upward-mobile persons. Contemporary preoccupation with the problem of neurotic ambition is reflected in numerous newspaper articles. One, entitled "Many Parents Use Their Children as Pawns in Status-Seeking Game," reads in part as follows:

The problem comes, of course, when parents' aspirations are too high, too anxiety-ridden, or too unrealistic for their children. Such aspirations, if thwarted, may keep a graduating student from seeking meaningful post-secondary vocational education—in which he might meet with a series of success experiences—and being forced instead into education for "prestige" occupations at the college level where he might meet with only frustration, anxiety, failure.

"Parents often keep their children from getting meaningful post-secondary education," reports a Georgia education researcher, "because they aspire to educational experiences linked with associated status either from the school preparing the student or from the field in which the student is training" (*Atlanta Constitution*, April 2, 1968).

Family Weekly for April 7, 1968, carried a piece entitled "Rod Steiger —The Star Who Has Everything—Almost," which says:

His Oscar competitor, Spencer Tracy, was beloved by all of Hollywood. But Rod has been described as "basically a very lonely man" and tempermental and hard to work with. Rod admits, "Most actors are so much in love with themselves that they haven't room left to love anyone else. I seem to be no exception.". . .

Asked what he still wants out of life, Rod Steiger replies sadly, "The ability to love more openly." Here is a man who can exhibit any emotion, including love, in front of an audience of any size—except possibly an audience of one.

The spirit of the foregoing citations has, of course, been neatly caught and dramatized by the hippies, with their devaluation of work and their exaltation of love. Although they commonly carry both of these postures to absurdity, their bifurcated thrust is a significant one, which seems to express attitudes which are shared, in varying degrees, by broad segments of our contemporary adolescent and adult society.

A generation or two ago, schoolchildren commonly read Longfellow's poem "Excelsior," the first verse of which goes as follows:

The shades of night were falling fast,
As through an Alpine village passed
A youth, who bore, 'mid snow and ice,
A banner with the strange device—
Excelsior!

In the next four verses, the youth is warned—by an old man, a peasant, a group of monks—of the perils that lie ahead; and a maiden says: "O stay and rest thy weary head upon this breast." But the youth, with a tear "in his bright blue eye," presses on! And the poem ends:

> A traveller, by the faithful hound,
> Half-buried in the snow was found,
> Still grasping in his hand of ice
> That banner with the strange device,
>   Excelsior!
>
> There in the twilight cold and gray,
> Lifeless, but beautiful, he lay
> And from the sky, serene and far,
> A voice fell, like a falling star—
>   Excelsior!

For a nation still intent upon subduing nature, fighting Indians, developing agriculture, industry, and science, and generally pushing forward the national frontier, this poem had great appeal as an ode to ambition and the spirit of do-or-die. But now that we have been rewarded for our heroic efforts by soil erosion, polluted air, streams, and rivers, shrinking natural resources, blighted cities, technological unemployment and poverty pockets, racial, political, and economic unrest, increasing delinquency and drug addiction, and other assorted evils, readers of "Excelsior," if there are any today, are less likely to be impressed that the youth got his banner to the top of the mountain than by the fact that he killed himself in the process. There is a new interest in people and their cultivation and fulfillment as human beings, and decidedly less concern with things and the status their mere possession supposedly bestows.

Longfellow's poem usefully reminds us that one can become alienated, estranged, "lost" by going to the mountaintop as well as by retreating into a cave in the valley.

One of the most remarkable and, I believe, historically significant movements of our time is the development of *small groups*, formed with various special objectives in mind (such as overcoming alcoholism or obesity) but all offering a greater opportunity for *social interest* or a sense of being interested in, liking, and related to several other persons in a way not provided, at least for these particular persons, by any of the more established primary social groups such as home, church, school, or neighborhood. In one way or another these various small groups help their members develop and experience social interest, with a resulting reduction in a wide variety of symptomatic (anxiety-controlling) behavior. Jackson [5] compiled a directory of such groups or organizations and found no less than 270 of them in existence in this country at that time. Drakeford [3] has described in some detail seven of the better known organizations of this kind: TOPS (Take Off Pounds Sensibly), Recovery, Inc., Alcoholics Anonymous, Seven Steppers (for ex-convicts), Synanon Foundation and Daytop Village, Inc. (for drug addicts), and Integrity Therapy. The December issue of *Coronet Magazine*, 1969, carries an article by Sagarin [9] entitled *The Outgroups: Organizations of Deviants in a Nation of Joiners*. And early in 1970, Hurvitz [4] will publish an article entitled "The Characteristics of Peer Self-Help Psychotherapy Groups and Their Implications for the Theory and Practice of Psychotherapy." At the end of his article Hurvitz lists the national headquarters' addresses of twelve organizations of the kind under discussion.

Thus it is clear that the traditional goals of individual achievement and material success have not been deeply satisfying and emotionally adequate for many modern men and women, and there is a widespread attempt to find ways in which adults can belatedly develop and enjoy the benefits of social interest and more meaningful interaction.

The foregoing considerations lead to the question: What can be done in the education of children and youth so that they will be less driven by the goal of personal accomplishment and more abundantly endowed with social interest and thus predisposed to better mental health? After noting that conventional types of education for mental health had, to date, not been very successful, Nikelly [7] suggests greater *actualization of social interest*. He states:

> The mental health sciences have hitherto been unable to contribute a universally palatable formula that can also be adaptable, simple, and meaningful to everyone in our democratic social system. The concept of social interest would seem to be the key to such an approach to mental health education. It becomes effective when combined with a fuller appreciation of the teleological and phenomenological factors involved in human behavior.
> 1. The inner aspects of the personality are often shaped and geared to outer goals that have social relevance of which the individual may be totally unaware. These goals are formed according to his perception of himself and the world. His behavior changes when such goals become conscious and understood by him. Said in another

way, the individual is made aware of the meaning of his behavior in relation to his outer goals, rather than being made familiar with "repressed" material. He can set his own objectives and consider them independent of repressed forces or "drives." The person can thus feel equipped to manage many of his problems without doubts that there may be aspects of himself over which he has little control.

2. Behavior anomalies are essentially characterized by an inability to deal with social reality, a lack of communal cooperation, and unpreparedness for social living. The issue becomes clear as one responds to the fundamental questions: "How much do others gain from my behavior?" "Do my actions enhance others?" By nature, man is a social being, and it is social feeling that has to be cultivated. Religion has already made such an attempt.

. . . There is much evidence that good adjustment depends upon and varies with the amount of social interest. Psychosis, for example, the severest of the mental illnesses, presents a picture of minimal social interest. Although at first seemingly superficial, the treatment, especially of the milder behavior disorders, for developing social interest, can have wider applicability than so-called "deeper" treatments. Such treatment is essentially a teaching for social living which can be applied early in life as a preventive measure.

3. Social interest is undoubtedly a simple concept, but it is simple ideas that people understand most effectively. If mental health education is to concern all people of all levels, it should not require technical terms. Its purpose, unlike specialization in a particular academic field, is to impart a lucid perspective for finding the meaning of life for man and his society. When the mental health sciences have transformed social interest into an emotional and cognitive reality, their chief aim will have been attained.

4. It can well be assumed that there is a need for the individual to feel significant. This need can be positive or negative from the viewpoint of society. The positive form does not imply wanting to be important in the ordinary sense, but rather an individual's attitude of co-feeling—how others value him, what he means to them. It is only when his actions are benign and propitious to others that he becomes significant to them. Likewise, a feeling of fitting into the social maze enhances one's sense of personal worthiness insofar as others are enriched and benefited by one's actions. Behavior disorders can be looked upon as the striving for antisocial significance and private rather than socially oriented goals. Such disorders are manifestations of a faulty outlook on life and of erroneous self-concepts.

The aim of education for mental health will be achieved when it is bound up with social interest—training people to fulfill their need for significance while thinking of others in their interpersonal relationships. "Social interest," according to Adler, "is the true and inevitable compensation for all the natural weaknesses of individual human beings" including feelings of inferiority that everyone seems to experience.

Ohlsen [8] had just published a book entitled *Group Counseling* which, although not specifically Adlerian in orientation, will, nevertheless, I believe go far toward fulfilling the objectives which Nikelly so vividly and persuasively outlines. The Ohlsen book is intended as a textbook for high school and college counselors who will use group, rather than individual, counseling methods, which are well designed to increase social interest and interpersonal skills of a positive and very valuable type. Alfred Adler was a true pioneer and prophet in emphasizing the neurosis-inducing effect of ambition, competition and accomplishment orientation, and in understanding that man, as Aristotle long ago observed, is truly a *social being* and cannot even approximate self-fulfillment when the social dimension of his existence is underdeveloped or distorted.

REFERENCES

1. Adler, A.: *The Individual Psychology of Alfred Adler.* Edited by H. L. and Rowena R. Ansbacher. New York, Basic Books, 1956.
2. Adler, A.: *The Problem of Neurosis.* (Originally published in 1929.) New York, Harper & Row, 1964.
3. Drakeford, J. W.: *Farewell to the Lonely Crowd.* Waco, Texas, Word Books, 1969.
4. Hurvitz, N.: Peer self-help psychotherapy groups and their implications for psychotherapy. *Psychotherapy: Theory, Research, and Practice,* 7:41–49, 1970.
5. Jackson, M. P.: *Their Brother's Keepers.* Urbana, Illinois, 1962, (mimeographed—out of print).
6. Mowrer, O. H.: New directions in the understanding and management of depression. In C. J. Frederick (Ed.): *The Future of Psychotherapy.* Boston, Little, Brown & Co., 1969.
7. Nikelly, A. G.: Social interest: a paradigm for mental health education. *J Individ Psychol,* 18:147–150, 1962.
8. Ohlsen, M.: *Group Counseling.* New York, Holt, Rinehart and Winston, 1969.
9. Sagarin, E.: The outgroups. *Coronet,* 7:131–161, 1969.
10. Warner, W. L.: *Yankee City.* New Haven, Yale University Press, 1963.

2

EXISTENTIAL-HUMANISM IN ADLERIAN PSYCHOTHERAPY

Edward A. Dreyfus and Arthur G. Nikelly

THE APPROACH TO THERAPY closest to Adler's is existential-humanism—a term which describes the therapist's attitude and stance toward the client. While existentialism tries to understand man as he exists and experiences his own world, humanism is concerned with man's relationship with his environment. Existential-humanism, then, is concerned with man's relation to himself—his feelings, thoughts, guilt, anguish, joy, loves—*and* man's relation with his world and others. It maintains that man, especially in psychotherapy, can be understood by himself alone but also in relationship to his fellow man. While existential-humanism understands man's essential aloneness, it also recognizes his dependence upon others.

Existential-humanistic psychotherapy involves a profound concern with the human condition. It is concerned with man's current place in his personal world as well as his relation to the world of others. The present experience becomes the focus. It views man as unique, with his own extraordinary "lifestyle," and capable of determining his own goals. Man is perceived as a rational, feeling, emerging organism capable of making choices and accepting the responsibility for them. What is more, man is seen as a growing organism who will choose continued growth if not thwarted and frustrated. It recognizes that the struggle toward self-actualization is the basic human motive and that man feels guilt when he fails to move in this direction—the guilt of unauthentic behavior. Subsequently, he may develop a variety of coping devices to deal with this unauthenticity, devices which may include making choices which limit his freedom, despite the fact that this action may yield still greater discomfort. Man must act, for choice without action is meaningless.

The following is a brief summary of an existential view of man:

> . . . man is seen as born anxious in an unknown world. He moves into the world in the face of this existential anxiety. Each time he moves into the unknown he experiences anxiety. As he moves he is constantly emerging into a unique being. At first, he reacts to the world in terms of his feelings. With the development of cognition he becomes conscious of his feelings and is capable of choosing a course of action. He is free to choose among many action-possibilities as his consciousness expands. While he has freedom of choice, he is also responsible for these choices. He is responsible for all his behavior and hence his own existence. The combined interplay of affect and cognition will, in part, determine his uniqueness. When he commits himself to a choice, he stands alone, singularly responsible for that choice. Failure to move, acting contrary to his feelings or thoughts, precluding choice, all leave man experiencing guilt for being unauthentic. When man realizes that he is being unauthentic, when he has so limited his choices, when he feels uncomfortable enough to the extent that he is unable to realize his potential, he seeks help.[2]

Persons who enter the psychotherapist's office do so because they experience discomfort with their present mode of being. They find that they perceive inadequate action-possibilities, limited possibilities, or an inundation of possibilities with little or no grounds for taking effective action. Often an inundation of possibilities is worse than the experience of no choice, for it leaves one panicked.

The task of the therapist is to try to understand both the real and apparent world of the client—to understand the client's world through the client's eyes. The therapist demonstrates his concern for the client and tries to assist him in gaining a greater clarity of perception in order that he can make more effective choices. Many times clients are unable to verbalize their anger, guilt, love, dependence, despair, and loneliness. The therapist, if he is seeing the world through the eyes of the client, can demonstrate an understanding and a willingness to share in these feelings without fear or judgement. Such a human relationship permits the client to explore his own feelings without trepidation.

The existential-humanistic position maintains that the relationship between client and therapist is the single most important therapeutic variable.[3] Adler [1] made a similar point when he stated that psychotherapists often help their clients not through their "methods" but by providing their clients a good human relationship. Openness and mutuality are two characteristics of this relationship that serve to increase the trust which is so necessary for effective psychotherapy. The therapist must demonstrate a genuine respect for the client as a person, for the client allows the therapist to enter his world by virtue of coming to the therapist's office. He does this even though he *knows* that allowing the therapist to enter his world will force him to move from the known to the unknown with all of the attendant anxiety of such a move. Although the client experiences discomfort in his own world, it is a more comfortable world than the unknown. Gradually, however, the client shrinks further and further from the real world in an attempt to protect himself from experienced threat. As he cuts himself off from new experiences, he further experiences the anxiety and guilt arising from an unauthentic existence. He may also cut himself off from the therapist, and the therapist must work against this withdrawal. He offers his being as the client struggles with trust. Such trust, when it occurs, allows the therapist to enter the client's world; as he enters, the client must move —change, and, thus, expand his world.

The therapist exhibits a deep sense of empathy toward the client and tries to experience his world. The client relives significant past experiences with the therapist and experiences a deep and meaningful relatedness with him. The therapist must be willing to involve himself with the client in this most intimate of relationships, for the problem of intimacy is often central to the client's existence.

The therapist must be able to understand the world of the client—the way he perceives things and the language he uses during the therapeutic situation—and he must be able to communicate in the same way as the client communicates with him. He must also have a facility for understanding metaphor, for a great deal of the client's talk is in metaphor. Once the central themes of the client's life are expressed, he is in a better position to execute his choices.

A client usually experiences distance between himself and others, and in many ways the therapeutic encounter is a test of closeness and intimacy. The client may want intimate relatedness, but he is also desperately afraid of it. Through his closeness with the therapist, the client may find it necessary to relinquish the very symptoms he so tenaciously holds. Many of these symptoms serve to keep the client from being truly known. He wants to be known; yet, he fears this experience, for if he is known he can be hurt even more through rejection. In a therapeutic paradox the client perpetuates the very symptoms which keep him from resolving his concern, and, consequently, the therapist must be willing to engage in "creative conflict" with the client.

As pointed out elsewhere,[4] ". . . existential-humanistic psychotherapy and Adlerian psychology agree on the importance of a human relationship, where there is cooperation between patient and therapist, where each is trying to understand the other's world." In Adler's[1] terms, psychotherapy is an "exercise in cooperation."

The existential-humanist is quite aware of his own impact during the therapeutic encounter. He continuously shares his own feelings, thoughts, and images as they are evoked by the client. He accepts responsibility for his impact and feels that this impact is an essential part of therapy. Too many therapists try to keep at a professional distance through fear of involvement; while keeping distant, they expect clients to come close or to be "accused" of resistance. The client is placed in a double-bind: the therapist says closeness is good but remains distant. What is the client to believe? The existential-humanist insists that the therapist fully participate in the therapy of the client, and participation may mean a loss of distinction between the roles of client and therapist. It may even mean a loss of professional stance and control; indeed, the client may well be in control as he leads the therapist through a melange of feelings, thoughts, distortions, and fears. Further, client control may be necessary for effective therapy, for how can the client follow the implicit suggestion of the therapist to control his own life, if the therapist will not permit him to begin to exercise such control during the therapeutic hour? The therapist's desire to control serves to foster the very dependence that the client is so desperately trying to relinquish. In a truly human encounter, each participant relinquishes control at one time or another—the lover and the beloved. The more the therapist assumes an omniscient, godlike role, the less he is able to engage in intimate relations in his own life.

In existential-humanistic psychotherapy, the therapist believes that the client has the answers to his current concerns, not the therapist. The client must determine the pace at which therapy moves and the goals that are to be set. The therapist adheres to the notion that each person has the goal of realizing his full potential to the best of his ability and that he continues in treatment because he is "getting something out of it." The therapist does not assume sole responsibility for what happens in therapy or for the continuation of treatment; rather, he believes that the solutions to the client's problems in living lie within himself. Although the therapist may assist the client in discovering these solutions, psychotherapy can be only as effective as the client wants it to be.

Obviously, psychotherapy is a collaborative effort on the part of two individuals, one of whom is designated therapist and the other, client or patient. Actually, the words consultant and consultee might be more appropriate, since the doctor-patient notion inherently connotes sickness and the idea that one person is going to heal the other. To assume that one person heals the other also presupposes that one person takes responsibility for the other. The existentially oriented therapist does not assume responsibility for the client; the client is responsible for himself. To assume otherwise would violate the integrity of the client and foster a kind of dependency which would only inhibit growth.

The psychotherapist does not *do* psychotherapy; rather, psychotherapy is a living, human encounter. The therapist does not change the client; rather, change occurs when the client feels understood. Psychotherapy occurs when at least two persons are engaged in the process of getting to know at least one person who is having difficulty in realizing his potential. Each participant in this collaborative effort gets to know the other, and each grows. It is assumed that such an engagement, with its attendant understanding and intimacy, will allow for an awareness and examination of increased action-possibilities.

If the therapist fears involvement in the world of the client, the latter senses that something is wrong and, therefore, relinquishes or suppresses his real feelings so that the therapist will not abandon him. Men desperately fear abandonment, for rejection and separation are experienced as tantamount to death or nonbeing, and will do almost anything to avoid this feeling.

Human problems are created through interaction, and only through human interaction can persons resolve these concerns. There is nothing fearful, bad, or sick about what the human being experiences. Most of man's problems stem from his perception of his relationships with others or his perception of himself. Hence, in the form of psychotherapy we are describing, only truly human modes of interacting are involved. The client through therapy can explore all of those aspects of human interaction which take place between himself and another person. He confronts his own feelings with respect to another person and meets the true feelings of the other person. The therapist, in response to the client, becomes involved in this interaction.

For the most part, the client comes to the therapist's office hoping to go on a trip, not a hallucinogenic trip, but a human trip. He is asking the therapist to take this trip with him, for he is afraid. He knows, however, that he is uncomfortable in the place where he currently is and that he would like the therapist to accompany him elsewhere. Neither the therapist nor the client knows where they will end up, and both are anxious as they move from the known to the unknown. As the trip begins, the client is the leader; he decides what shall be talked about and describes the lay of the land. Gradually, as the therapist sees that the client has a feeling for the terrain, he gently guides the client to look at other areas. The roles of leader and follower soon disappear, and at any given time the client or therapist may assume either role. On occasion, the two may get lost as they explore.

Two of the most important kinds of human relatedness which frequently occur during psychotherapy are encounter and confrontation. These, in addition to the psychotherapist's basic humanness, are the tools of the existential-humanist. The encounter refers to the genuinely personal interaction between two persons, any two persons, including client and therapist. It is a meeting of two human beings concerned with more effective communication, where one is genuinely concerned with the well-being of the other. There is no essential difference between the two people with the exception that one has sought the other. The therapist works *with* his client and does not view him as an object to be manipulated or exploited. The therapist's role must be transcended by his own humanness. During the encounter both participants are equally free to express their feelings, attitudes, and thoughts. The therapist allows the client's world to unfold during the therapeutic encounter but does not probe into the past, since he views the present as a reflection of the past. The therapist holds that the past can be understood in terms of the present rather than the present, in terms of the past. The client's problems are viewed as being in the present; the past is relevant only as it emerges into the present. The therapist gleans a picture of the client's world as the client feels free to disclose it during the encounter. There is mutual sharing during the process: the client shares his world, and the therapist shares his feelings and impressions. The openness and mutuality that exists between client and therapist is the encounter, where each feels understood. The humanness which occurs as an integral part of the encounter permits the client to become more aware of his own humanity and to realize the uniqueness of his own existence.

Confrontation involves being faced with a choice regarding one's own existence. The therapist confronts the client with an aspect of the latter's world, and the client must choose whether or not he will respond and what his response will be. Confrontation implies a direct encounter of the client with himself and/or the therapist on issues of the client's existence. His integrity and dignity are not at stake during the confrontation, but the issue is.

The therapist's role during the confrontation is active. He stays with the client throughout the confrontation, even though the two may argue violently. The resolution of the conflict may even bring these two struggling human beings closer. The relationship deepens, as the therapist becomes committed completely to the client.

It should be clear from the foregoing that the therapist cannot give meaning or purpose to a client's life; he cannot answer the client's questions about his own existence. The therapist must, however, stay with the client as the latter explores and struggles with these questions. He can share his own concerns and solutions, but he must not imply that these are the only alternatives. The therapist encourages the client to explore alternative modes of being and to seek unique solutions to present concerns. Many clients want to emulate the therapist; sensing that he has come to grips with life, they feel that what is good for the therapist is good for them. While the therapist may be flattered by this reinforcement, it must be avoided since it serves only to limit the client's choices and to help him avoid responsibility. The client must freely choose a unique lifestyle rather than model his behavior after the therapist. Thus, unlike other forms of therapy, the therapist does not offer himself as a model but confronts the client with his own behavior in order that the client may realize his own philosophy of life and unique mode of being.

Human concerns are best understood in human terms and most

problems can be resolved through the interaction of human beings. Techniques will not "cure" anyone, but a recognition and understanding of another's experience, coupled with a genuine willingness to explore, offers new possibilities for resolution.

REFERENCES

1. Adler, A.: *Superiority and Social Interest.* Edited by H. L. and Rowena R. Ansbacher. Evanston, Ill., Northwestern University Press, 1964, pp. 7–9.
2. Dreyfus, E. A.: Humanness: A therapeutic variable. *Personnel Guid J,* 45:573–578, 1967.
3. Dreyfus, E. A.: An existential approach to counseling. In C. Beck (Ed.): *Guidelines for Guidance,* Dubuque, Iowa, Wm. C. Brown, 1966, pp. 417–427.
4. Dreyfus, E. A.: Humanness and psychotherapy: a confirmation. *J Indiv Psychol,* 24:82–85, 1968.

3

FUNDAMENTAL CONCEPTS OF MALADJUSTMENT

Arthur G. Nikelly

The client is not born maladjusted; he becomes maladapted in the course of his psychological and social development. As a child amidst strong adults, helplessness is imprinted on him but should diminish gradually as he finds a place for himself in adult society. If he is uncertain about himself in relation to his world, he may utilize unrealistic, subjective impressions of life and people in order to distort, conceal, or compensate for his unexpressed and often unconscious feelings of inferiority and incompleteness. Consequently, maladjustment can be characterized as the client's misdirected goal of achieving an apparent superiority in order to overcome feelings of inferiority. Instead of adopting a healthy mode of human interaction, however, he achieves this goal by demonstrating a malfunction of his personality which adversely affects himself and others. Although he desires security and contentment, he attempts to attain it, paradoxically, by means which are socially detrimental and damaging to himself. In the final analysis, he either uses others through inadequacy or withdraws from life tasks and people.

Living is not a static condition but a form of *movement* toward subjectively formed goals which, for most persons, are within reason and the domain of reality. In case of maladjustment, individuals espouse fictional and unrealistic objectives in order to attain a sense of security, but the apparent advantage they obtain is not bound up with the interests of society and offers only transient relief and a false sense of

21

control over others. An inevitable conflict rises between self and others which expresses itself in anxiety, depression, withdrawal, underachievement, antisocial behavior, or psychosomatic symptoms.

Some of the causes for maladjustment are as follows: 1) *Parental overprotection* tends to make the child feel inadequate and unaccepted by denying him the opportunity to become independent and responsible. He may attempt to compensate for these feelings of inadequacy through demonstrations of aggression which his parents and other adult surrogates may intensify through suppression. As a young adult, he may express his anger not only to his parents but to his teachers and to other members of the community at large. They, in turn, may reject him and heighten his feelings of isolation and inferiority. The situation may worsen, since he is likely to be treated as a "sick" person who has a "disease" that must be "treated." 2) *Parental pampering* develops an attitude of dominance in the child, regardless of the parents' education or economic status. When the child learns that he cannot always obtain what he desires, he is apt to become rebellious and hostile. 3) *Parental neglect* may cause a child to see others as demanding and unfriendly and to become incapable of social cooperation. Such a child may exhibit an excessive need for appreciation and love but be unable to elicit these feelings from others. 4) *Parental partiality* often results in a power contest between siblings. The life pattern of the less favored sibling may alter radically, even becoming diametrically opposed to that of the other sibling. 5) *Physical unattractiveness or a handicap,* whether actual, exaggerated, or imaginary, may dominate an individual's life pattern and cause him to rebel or to withdraw from others. On the other hand, he may exhibit inadequacy as a means of forcing others to help him. 6) *Parental domination* may produce reactions similar to those generated by overprotection. The child often views authority figures as unfriendly and develops disobedient behavior.[1]

Maladjustment is based primarily on the client's false conclusions about his experiences and from significant facts in his life (sibling rivalry, rejecting mother, pampering father, physical debility) which in themselves did not cause his maladjustment but served to trigger his thinking in a certain direction. In other words, he selected those elements from his environment which fit a subjectively conceived goal. Once the client has a mistaken opinion of himself, he cannot relate effectively with reality and meet social demands without feeling insecure. Since his estimation of himself is inaccurate and fictional, his actions are bound to be misdirected. Since he overvalues or underestimates himself, he is unprepared to meet the exigencies of real life and unwittingly safeguards his threatened self-esteem through aggression or withdrawal. In the final analysis, selfishness is characteristic of any type of maladjustment since the client gives priority to self-esteem above the esteem and objectives of his kin-group or the society at large. The apperception of the maladjusted person is self-bound, and he ignores or distorts the needs of his milieu. Only when his own and society's needs coalesce can he be called well adjusted.

In dealing with maladjustment, the therapist must realize that the client responds to life as a *whole* person. Personality cannot be fragmented into emotions, egos, needs, impulses, the unconscious; rather, the therapist must perceive the relationship between personality and the client's ultimate *goals*. Emotions may emerge or recede depending upon objectives of which the client may be only dimly aware. Negative attitudes and social misconduct may be defined through the client's intentions, which as yet remain unverbalized. The client may resort to forgetfulness to hide intent or rely on guilt feelings to make transgressions appear less demeaning and to avoid responsibility. Although the client may see personality variables as the reasons for his problems, such aspects of personality are in themselves meaningless unless related by the therapist to the client's goals and intentions.[4]

Human behavior must be understood within a *social* context. Since the client, like everyone, relates first with his family and then with the larger society, the therapist may be seen, theoretically, as a mother substitute who continues to foster the child's independence and responsibility. Since social striving, coupled with a quest for personal significance, is considered the strongest factor in human motivation, the client's subjective interpretation of the social consequences of his actions is the deciding factor in his adjustment. Every person needs to feel *esteemed* and *wanted*, but his interpretations of situations involving himself and others are colored with personal meaning and subjective reasoning which may prevent him from fulfilling these needs in spite of honest and concerted efforts. Every person needs to feel that he has *control*—that he can master certain situations and exercise restraint over others. The degree of control an individual regards as necessary depends upon his opinion of himself and upon his definition of control. For some, being in control means a sense of security; for others, being in control requires a position of superiority and an exaggerated conviction of self-value and merit. A person who identifies with the goals of his social community will not seek to dominate others through self-aggrandizement or other forms of maladjustment. On the one hand, a client's quest for a subjectively conceived position of success or superiority may be denied through unrealistic expectations or attained through excessive fantasy life or antisocial actions. On the other hand, the client strives toward *social interest* and, ideally, this social striving may be combined with the desire for personal success and result in maturity and mental health. In other words, the client's need to feel superior is divested in the services of society. Social interest, the opposite of loneliness and alienation, implies an intimate belonging to the human race and a positive contribution to its goals.

Goals and values are subjectively created by everyone through the individualized interpretation of personal experiences, and maladjustment occurs when these interpretations form a distorted image of self and environment. On the basis of these perceptions, insecurity and fear may develop. An individual may lose courage and self-esteem and may *compensate* by exhibiting exaggerated behavioral manifestations such as uncooperativeness, withdrawal, passivity, alcoholism, obsessive fears, or depression. Compensation in a person's behavior can be desirable when fused with the interests of society but results in maladjustment when the individual is making up for something which is based on a false conclusion about himself or stems from an erroneous perception of others and their reactions toward him. He is afraid to try new experiences which may lead to an adjustment to the environment and expends energy on useless actions. His compensatory behavior, then, is inappropriate or out of proportion to the real situation.

Symptoms normally convey a hidden *purpose* of which the client is unaware.[2] He may wish to stave off responsibility and involvement or to elicit a reaction from others which has private meaning. This meaning often has to do with the advantage the client feels he has over others when he behaves differently. These social misconceptions and private distortions are explored with the therapist who tries to understand how they enhance the client's self-esteem or lessen his feelings of inadequacy. Maladjustment will normally recede as the client's faulty view of himself and of his world is understood through exploration and therapy.

Although this process is not synonymous with depth analysis, it may prove a lengthy and arduous task for the client and therapist to examine the current context of the client's interactions and to understand the nature of his maladjustment. Conflicts "within" are essentially connected with those with whom he interacts. His relationships with others and his perceptions of them clarify his self-image, his goals, and his behavior. The therapist must emphasize that the client has the freedom to choose between alternatives and is responsible for his behavior. His actions occur not because of his environment or biological inheritance, but despite them. He reacts independently of these factors since he either rejects or *uses* them, depending upon his purposes and intentions. If the symptoms work for him, they become entrenched and fused with his life pattern. If this life pattern is creating problems, psychological help becomes necessary. The therapist is then expected to uncover the client's life pattern, to demonstrate to him that this pattern is based on false premises and, consequently, is disadvantageous for him and must be altered.[3]

REFERENCES

1. Adler, A.: *The Individual Psychology of Alfred Adler.* Edited by H. L. and Rowena R. Ansbacher. New York, Basic Books, 1956, pp. 366–371.
2. Adler, A.: *The Science of Living.* Edited by H. L. Ansbacher. Garden City, Doubleday, 1969, pp. 1–4.
3. Adler, A.: *Superiority and Social Interest.* Edited by H. L. and Rowena R. Ansbacher. Evanston, Ill., Northwestern University Press, 1964. pp. 191–201.
4. Ansbacher, H. L.: The structure of individual psychology. In B. B. Wolman (Ed.): *Scientific Psychology.* New York, Basic Books, 1965, pp. 340–364.

4

BASIC PROCESSES IN PSYCHOTHERAPY

Arthur G. Nikelly

ONE OF THE fundamental assumptions of psychotherapy is that the client is not a passive recipient of stimuli or experiences from without, but is instead, an active participant who reacts to others uniquely, interpreting their actions and behavior in his own subjective and idiosyncratic way. Clinical experience demonstrates repeatedly that biological, instinctual, or constitutional factors are not decisive; rather, it is the individual's attitude toward them—what use he makes of them —that will determine his behavior. Independent of these factors, he originates and produces an attitude, which he may use either positively or negatively, depending on which attitude will give him the most self-esteem or control over others. Better therapeutic results are obtained, then, when the emphasis is on the individual's immediate and unique manner of perceiving and interpreting his experiences rather than on the nature of the experiences themselves.

A conceptual understanding of maladjustment, then, is linked operationally with the client's interpersonal processes. Unacceptable behavior cannot be understood as an isolated fragment; instead, it must be understood in terms of the client's total life pattern as he moves toward a purpose of which he may not always be fully aware. If he can be helped to understand exactly what he is doing and to acknowledge responsibility for his behavior, he can become conscious of his capacity for change and be further supported and guided. Consequently, to understand and to treat maladjustment, the therapist should deal di-

27

rectly with things as they are, rather than with things as they should or might be, or exclusively as they *have* been.

The client's difficulties or symptoms always have *social* meaning, and it is within this context that the therapist must understand the client's behavior. Maladjustment occurs when the individual has been prevented from experiencing and absorbing the elements of his social milieu and, consequently, depends upon an interactional process. As in a dialogue or a play, two or more persons are required for a meaningful interaction. The therapist, then, seeks to discover what prevented the client from benefiting from his experiences during the course of his development, what in the process of socialization hampered the sense of responsibility and social feelings which are necessary for a successful adjustment to life.

A distinction must be made at this point between counseling and psychotherapy.[2] The counseling procedure involves the client's understanding of his immediate situation and the solving of a problem which affects him and others. No attempt is made to effect a fundamental change of the client's personality. On the other hand, psychotherapy involves the client's reorientation and requires insight into his life style as well as his motives, attitudes, and values. Psychotherapy is of a longer duration and is not limited to the supportive techniques of counseling. When a person needs reorientation to a particular situation, counseling is indicated. If the problem is of a long-standing duration, psychotherapy is recommended.

Dreikurs systematized Adler's technique of therapy by distinguishing four essential but overlapping stages in the therapeutic process which are applicable to all types of maladjustment.[3] These stages do not necessarily follow the same order and often vary in emphasis and length depending upon the client. These phases are more or less present in all existing therapies. The first stage sets the pace of communication and establishes rapport between therapist and client. A trusting relationship of mutual cooperation and respect and an agreement on objectives is established. In the second stage the client's current behavior, as he experiences it, is examined and with it his whole life situation (birth order, family atmosphere, early recollections) in an attempt to identify a common denominator from these characteristics. The emphasis in this phase is on investigating and uncovering. During the third stage the therapist extracts from these characteristics an underlying pattern of behavior and explains it to the client. The client's fundamental approach to life is interpreted to him. In the fourth stage the client is encouraged to work through his problem and to implement his insights. It is considered to be the most significant stage for eliciting behavior change. The aim of the last phase is either to change the mistaken goals of the immediate situation (counseling) or to modify the basic personality and lifestyle of the client (psychotherapy). In either case, the goal is to reorient the client through encouragement. An attempt will be made in the following paragraphs to spell out some details of technique relevant to these four phases.

Since the client's basic character is revealed through his personal interactions, the therapist must carefully observe the client's behavior and attitude in this new situation from the very first encounter. The client's disposition to control the situation through undue assertiveness or passivity should not be overlooked. An equal and cooperative relationship must be maintained between therapist and client to produce an effective, operational dialogue. The therapist is not an omnipotent healer, neither is the client a passive recipient to be changed by an agent outside himself. The client is encouraged to tell his problem as he sees it and to offer possible reasons for his difficulties, reasons which reveal his private thinking. Factors beyond the immediate situation are also explored: his employment, family situation, interpersonal relationships, and other significant stress factors. The therapist probes for contributing elements beyond the symptoms which may serve as goals to be achieved or avoided through these symptoms. The bright college student who suddenly loses interest in his academic work or the woman who appears clumsy and naive when she is about to make decisions regarding impending marriage clearly indicates that anticipatory events are associated with current problems or reported distresses. When his aims and intentions become known to the client, they can be altered and the symptoms and problems will subsequently dissipate. The therapist must also observe the nonverbal expressions of the client, for these may be interpreted in much the same way as verbal expression. Inappropriate grins, giggling, facial grimaces, hand gestures, posture, and other physical manifestations may reflect the client's state of mind when he describes a particular situation. The therapist can interpret these expressive features as behavior samples which confirm the client's basic style of living.

The therapist sets the client at ease during the first interview by being relaxed and friendly; irrelevant or neutral comment may help to desensitize the client and lessen the tension. The therapist can further relieve the client's anxiety by explaining the purpose of the first interview: to identify the problem before agreeing upon the goals of therapy. He assures the client that his job is not to be critical or to make judgments but to understand why the client behaves the way he does. The therapist must learn to be a listener. His facial expression should convey respect and attention as well as interest. He must not interrupt, neither must he jump to conclusions. The therapist's answers and questions should be brief. He tries to say little and to give the client openings for further areas of discussion. The client must be allowed to state the problem the way he sees it, with his own opinions and subjective impressions. At the end of the evaluation session, the therapist may inquire whether he has neglected to ask about other aspects of the problem; the client should feel that he has said enough about himself.

The therapist does not agree or disagree with the client, though at the end of the session he may recapitulate what the client has said. He may repeat or reconstruct statements which the client has stated in a fragmentary fashion. The therapist may attempt to clarify the client's remarks by saying, "In other words, you feel that . . ." The client may then be able to restructure or rephrase the sentence as he wishes. When the client has difficulty expressing a conflict area, the therapist can indicate that he is well aware of the client's feelings.

All sessions cannot be conducted by one rigid formula. Verbal clients may talk a great deal without saying very much while other clients are able to communicate the problem as they see it in a very precise but adequate manner. The therapist should not make promises regarding results or the length of psychotherapy. Initially, the depth and breadth of the problem is assessed; later the nature, duration, and goals of therapy are discussed.

Instead of merely labeling the client as "immature," "impulsive," "schizoid," or "unpredictable," the therapist must decipher the *movement* and direction of the client's exhibited behavior. The client cannot be described as a static entity; rather, his behavior must be understood in terms of his unconscious goals. Therapy begins when the client determines the objectives he is trying to achieve (or understands those he is trying to avoid). We might think of the client, metaphorically, as a person who is running; besides asking what the client is running from, the therapist should help him understand what he is running toward.

Besides understanding the client's goals, the therapist must also understand the client's style of functioning. Instead of deciphering unconscious wishes and motives, as the psychoanalyst would do, the therapist looks for the basic pattern by which the client moves through life and tries to understand what has remained unchanged within the client since his formative years. This consistent pattern is known as the *lifestyle* and must be altered before any significant change can take place. The client must also understand his lifestyle as the therapist explains it to him. At first, the client may show anger or resist such an interpretation. If this happens, the therapist must explore these emotions with the client because they too are part of his lifestyle. The client's relation to the therapist is, in fact, a sample of his style of life.

The ideal therapeutic atmosphere encourages an egalitarian dialogue between client and therapist without detachment or anonymity. The client feels respected, belonging to a category of his own. The psychotherapist must be actively involved in the therapy. He should not be reluctant to show feeling during the therapeutic process. If he hides emotion which would be normally expected, he gives a deceptive and perhaps contaminated picture of himself to the client. If the therapist shows that he is human and fallible, the client will not imitate, adore, or worship the therapist. If the therapist remains merely passive, the client may respond accordingly and become apathetic and unproductive. Active involvement demonstrates that the therapist has the capacity to show social interest, and this social interest can in turn be expected of the client.

Any form of psychotherapy involves change in the client's cognitive attitudes as well as his feelings, and such change will ultimately be reflected in the client's value system. The therapist should not hesitate to disclose that he too has values and that his and the client's values may occasionally clash. Such a conflict can actually form a landmark during the process of psychotherapy because the client must examine his own values carefully in order to understand why they fail to help him function effectively as an emotionally healthy and adjusted person. The therapist must help the client determine what made him formulate values which are erroneous or self-defeating. Although value orientation may be secondary to emotional or intellectual orientation, a client's values can be dealt with directly and this action, in turn, may alter his attitudes and interpersonal perceptions.

After successful therapy the client demonstrates behavior change by the decrease of unwanted symptoms, by the strength of his realistic self-image, by increased cooperation and activity directed toward the welfare of others, and by his ability to act on his own initiative and to deal effectively on the interpersonal level. For such change to take place, the client must demonstrate an initial impetus for change by expressing some degree of cooperation with the therapist and by feeling equal with him. When this has been accomplished, the client is expected to act on his new insights outside the therapy situation.[1]

REFERENCES

1. Adler, A.: *The Individual Psychology of Alfred Adler.* Edited by H. L. and Rowena R. Ansbacher. New York, Basic Books, 1956, pp. 326–349.
2. Dreikurs, R.: The Adlerian approach to therapy. In M. I. Stein (Ed.): *Contemporary Psychotherapies.* Glencoe, Ill., Free Press, 1961, pp. 80–94.
3. Dreikurs, R.: Adlerian psychotherapy. In F. Fromm-Reichmann and J. L. Moreno (Eds.): *Progress in Psychotherapy.* New York, Grune & Stratton, 1956, pp. 111–118.

Part II   Assessment Techniques

5

FAMILY CONSTELLATION

Bernard H. Shulman and Arthur G. Nikelly

Family constellation is a term used to describe the socio-psychological configuration of a family group. The personality characteristics and emotional distance of each person, age differences, order of birth, the dominance or submission of each member, the sex of the siblings, and the size of the family are all factors in the family constellation and affect the development of the personality. The position of each child in the family constellation not only helps to determine his personality development but also enables the therapist to understand the client's personality dynamics. Certain behavior types can be characterized by examining the individual's place in the constellation. Thus, the first born, the second born, the third born, and the only child have certain characteristics which render their personality predictable in terms of attitudes, personality traits and subsequent behavior. Chapter 7, will present these implications more extensively.

Ordinal position is not a "cause" of behavior disturbance but a situation in which the child finds himself, a fact of life to which he responds. Five ordinal positions can be considered basic, and all other positions can be seen as variations, combinations, or permutations of these five. The five are identified as an only, eldest, second, middle, and youngest child. One child may occupy two positions (second and youngest child). A child may have been several years in one position and then find himself in another (a youngest child becomes a middle child or a middle child becomes a youngest child when a younger sibling dies). A child may be overrun by a younger sibling who is more intelligent, aggressive, or favored and may occupy an actual position different from his order of birth (an oldest child may function as a second or even as a youngest child). Similarly, an older child, by reason of physical illness or frailty, may "back into" the position of a youngest child.

Individuals occupying any of these five basic positions are considered to have their own characteristic attitudes which tend to remain fixed but which in turn may lead to a variety of behavioral reactions, compensatory or otherwise. Thus, two children in identical ordinal positions may behave in entirely different ways and may have different compensatory goals but will tend to have the same underlying attitude or *Weltanschaung.*

It is common knowledge that parents exert great influence on the developing child, whether the child sees them as models to be imitated or to be cast aside. Parental behavior is generally responsible for the *atmosphere* of the home—whether it is peaceful or warlike, cheerful or depressing. Through example, parents provide *dimensions of behavior* for their children.

When parents are very different from each other, they provide separate guide lines for the children to follow. Guide lines, then, may be clear and definite or confused and contradictory. In the latter case, it is difficult for the child to determine what he is supposed to be. The following chapter, "Family Atmosphere," describes these influences more fully.

Some family values are cultural, and are found throughout the community; others are individual and vary from family to family. Thus, one family may be patriarchal, another matriarchal. One family may exhibit open conflict, another may conceal conflict under a disguise or surface politeness. One family may demonstrate warmth, closeness, and mutual involvement, another may show cold, distant, and detached relationships. Dreikurs maintains that family pattern does not necessarily determine a person's specific type of behavior and can even produce opposite behavior among siblings. If moral concepts and value orientations are well defined and practiced by both parents, however, there is a greater likelihood that the children will follow a similar pattern. While such similarities of traits may reveal family atmosphere, differences in personality traits between siblings often reflect position in the family constellation.[1]

A child may react positively or negatively to the behavior of his parents. He may pattern himself after a parent or in opposition to a parent; he may select traits from each parent to emulate, always searching for values, attitudes, and techniques that enhance himself and increase his ability to cope with life. Since he knows nothing else, he must choose from what is available in the microcosm of the family. Much of this emulation and rejection takes place before the development of speech and frequently the child adapts or rejects a value or attitude without awareness that he is doing so. Divergence in behavior between siblings is often partly determined by competition between them. The second child may avoid the territory of the first. If, for example, the first born has patterned himself after one parent, the second child may choose to imitate those aspects of that dominant parent which the first born has overlooked or to imitate the other parent.

Ehrenwald [2] notes that attitudes occur in compounds or pairs. He makes the distinction between four major patterns of interaction: sharing, contagion, complementarity, and resistance. These patterns provide vehicles for the transmission of attitudes and traits from parent to child.

Ehrenwald goes on to explain that sharing and contagion are patterns of reacting against a trait, though in different ways. *Sharing* refers to the simple imitation of parental traits by the child while *contagion* refers to the "catching" of negative traits such as fearfulness or prejudices from the parent. A trait can be said to be shared when, for example, a child imitates a parent's tendency to be passive and self-effacing in relations with others. The behavior of the child always reflects some facet of parental attitude and family values, just as it reflects the child's own attitude and values. When one finds a "power drunk" child, one can safely assume that force and forcefulness has high value (either positive or negative) to at least one parent. The child who constantly opposes and fights his mother has a mother who constantly opposes and fights him. The child can be said to have "caught" the trait of opposition and the interest in power from his mother.

Resistance refers to the child's negative response to a particular parental trait and seems to be related to the Adlerian concept of *Gegenspieler* (the opponent) who chooses his patterns of behavior in response to the observed behavior of his opponent. He cannot freely choose what he wants to do until he knows what the other wants, since he can act only in opposition. His opposition may be in the form of overt defiance, negativism, passive-aggressive behavior, or conspicuous attempts to satisfy the opponent while secretly arranging to disappoint him.

Complementarity refers to many kinds of reciprocal relationships, healthy or unhealthy. A basic, enduring example of complementarity is the relation between the sexes; each brings something the other lacks. Parent and child can also complement each other. When we speak of complementary traits, we refer to traits which, while not imitative, permit peaceful transactions between child and parent. Such traits are demonstrated by the intellectual child who is a good student and has an uneducated parent who admires intellectual achievement. It is important to note, in this instance, that the *traits* are not imitated but the *values* are.

Another kind of parental influence is favoritism which may bestow both an advantage and a disadvantage on the favorite. He may have an undisputed place in the family, a place attended by prestige, and, consequently, he struggles less to make his mark and more quickly finds a place among others. He conforms more easily and expects to be accepted. The sibling who is not "the favorite" may never feel sure of being accepted, but the favored child may never learn to fight for his position or his cause and be unable to face a situation where he is not or cannot be the "favorite." The other sibling may learn early in life to accept "second-best" or to depend on himself and his own efforts without feeling discouraged by the unfriendliness of others.

Sex is accepted by all as an important determinant of personality. It is important to note that socially prescribed sexual role may have little to do with the biological functions of sex; rather, it is the sexual *role* that is important. The child decides what sexual role he will play; he may choose to fulfill the socially assigned role, to play the role of the opposite sex, to be neuter, to be a better example of his gender than anyone else, or to find another permutation of the sexual role that suits him. It is the child's conception of the sexual role and the positive and/or negative values he assigns to it that determine his response. The development of his values are influenced by the family constellation. In some families, one sex may be more highly regarded than the other; in others, one parent may provide an undesirable example of a particular sex or all the advantages may seem to accrue to one sex. Variations in the conceptions of the sexual roles are endless and follow the same laws of expediency and empirical value that all trait development follows. The child does what he believes work best for him or he chooses according to his values—his belief about what is important in life. If a little boy (and, later, the adult man) does not believe in his masculinity and fails to measure up to his own standard of maleness, he must, if he values maleness, compensate by striving to be more masculine than others, to prove his masculinity or at least to conceal his felt deficiency from others.

The keystone of Adlerian theory is that the child develops those traits that he believes will prove most useful to him in later life. He may not consider these traits ideal, but he has compromised with his limitations. A girl may desire to be strong and masculine while recognizing the impossibility of achieving such a goal. She may then struggle hard to acquire traits of compliance and submission because she believes that these traits will ultimately serve her best. She may, however, hold these same traits in contempt because of her private value system. The most powerful determinant in the family constellation is the child's own perception of what is needful for him. In the act of deciding what he needs, the child influences his future pattern of living and may make crucial mistakes that later cripple his endeavors.

The first step in eliciting the client's family constellation is to have him describe his siblings, noting their ages, the similarities and differences between himself and his siblings, and their positive and negative attributes. The emotional relationships between siblings and between each sibling and the parents are then explored to determine, for example, who the favorites were, who got along well with other family members, who was most quarrelsome, who was most punished. Finally, the client is asked to express his own feelings and attitudes toward other members of the family and to mention people outside the family who influenced it.

In discussion of his family, the client often reveals inconsistencies and subjective impressions which point to tendencies in his lifestyle. Domination, competition, oppositional tendencies, defiance, passivity, help-lessness, discouragement, personal habits, life expectations, and general sources of conflict can all be revealed through the study of the client's family constellation. The family constellation thus illuminates his present pattern of behavior in terms of values, attitudes, self-concepts, goals, and style of life. The value of the family constellation in diagnosis is discussed at greater length elsewhere by the senior author.[3]

If the client understands the experiences of his formative years, he can understand his present actions. He can perceive that he retains those traits that serve a present purpose and eliminates others that do not further present goals. Through reporting his position and interrelatedness in his family, the client also examines his social relatedness and his perception of himself.

REFERENCES

1. Dreikurs, R.: *Psychology in the Classroom.* New York, Harper, 1957, p. 9.
2. Ehrenwald, J.: Neurotic interaction and patterns of pseud-heredity in the family. *Amer J Psychiat, 115:*134–142, 1958.
3. Shulman, B.: The family constellation in personality diagnosis. *J Individ Psychol, 18:*35–47, 1962.

6

FAMILY ATMOSPHERE

Edith A. Dewey

While the family constellation describes the interaction between members of the family, family atmosphere or climate may be defined as the characteristic pattern established by parents and presented to their children as a standard for social living.[4] Since each person responds to a situation according to his own outlook on life,[1] family climate is not a direct causal agent in the development of personality; instead, the individual interprets the meaning and significance of the family atmosphere in the light of his own "biased apperception" or "faulty logic." [3] Typical family atmospheres which can give the therapist clues in understanding the child or adult client's behavior are presented below.[2] These atmospheres may produce typical patterns of behavior known as *lifestyles* and are described more fully in Chapter 11.

The *rejective* atmosphere makes an individual feel that he is not accepted, although this may not actually have been the case. Individuals who have had no experience in being loved and accepted are unable to love and accept others; those who do not trust others fail to develop self-trust. Sometimes parents reject one or all of their children, but in most cases parents love their children although they may find their behavior difficult to accept. Parents need help in learning to separate the *deed* from the *doer* and learn, to accept the child but reject his misbehavior, and to demonstrate this difference to the child. Frequently the "good" child in the family pushes another child down, and the parents may unwittingly reinforce the "bad" child's feelings of rejection. Their reactions may further discourage an already discouraged child. A teacher or counselor should examine the family constellation, especially in the case of a child who feels rejected. Usually a favored sibling is in the picture.

When there is absolute and unquestioned obedience in the family, the *authoritarian* atmosphere prevails. Children from such homes often rebel later in life and are apt to be inconsiderate of others, quarrelsome, unpopular, emotionally unstable, and more sensitive to praise and blame than children from more democratic family climates. Children raised in an authoritarian atmosphere are usually polite but are often shy and timid and have nervous habits, tics, and other evidence of stress and anxiety. The more conforming children are frequently unable to solve their own problems, constantly seek direction and rely on the decisions of others. They lack creativity, spontaneity, and resourcefulness. The more rebellious ones often resort to indirect and evasive responses including lying and stealing. Since they are untrained in handling freedom, they frequently "go wild" in an atmosphere of permissiveness and do things that they would not dare to do at home.

There is no strength greater than the strength of weakness! In the *martyrdom* atmosphere the "martyr" demonstrates how brutal others are and how "innocent" or "helpless" he is. The "martyr" [5] is actually a pessimist who has a low self-esteem and tries to ennoble himself by looking down on others and demonstrating the suffering he endures. He is critical of others, although his criticism may be veiled by good intentions and self-righteousness. He feels sorry for himself and believes life is unfair to him. Sometimes a martyr acts cheerfully and plays to his own audience as though he is above all others. Martyrs fulfill themselves by noble suffering. A prototype is the angelic alcoholic's wife who looks down on her no-good husband. If this marriage should end, she will find another "inferior" husband in order to continue her noble suffering. Should the alcoholic be cured of his problem, the spouse is likely to become disturbed. In the martyrdom atmospheres, a "martyr" lifestyle may also develop.

When discipline is erratic and routines are nonexistent, the child does not know what to expect of others or what is expected of him. An *inconsistent* atmosphere exists. It is well recognized that young children need kind but firm and consistent discipline and order in their lives. Variety and occasional surprises are beneficial, but these should be the exception rather than the usual order of the day. An atmosphere of inconsistency leads to instability, lack of self-control, lack of motivation, self-centeredness, a craving for excitement, and difficulties in work and human relationships.

The *suppressive* climate denies the freedom to express thoughts and feelings honestly. When a child is frequently reprimanded for saying what he thinks or how he feels ("It is naughty to hate your little sister!" "You must never say such things!") he may learn to "put up a front" and not admit how he actually feels. Sometimes he resorts to daydreaming and unrealistic fantasies. The "lost prince" fantasy is common: "I am not really their child but a famous person unrecognized. One day, when I am discovered, I'll be in command and then they will be sorry they treated me this way!" Children raised in this atmosphere often do not trust their own feelings and find it difficult to express personal thoughts and true feelings. They avoid close relationships with others and often have difficulty in the intimate relationship of marriage.

The *hopeless* atmosphere is characterized by discouragement and pessimism. In city slums and depressed rural areas an atmosphere of hopelessness is widespread. Parents in middle- or upper-class homes may also suffer severe discouragement, and children who feel defeated see little hope for themselves. Discouragement is highly contagious, and one who has a pessimistic outlook on life can usually find plenty of justification for his pessimism. Discouraged parents are usually unable to encourage their children, and therapists are very familiar with discouraged clients. This hopelessness can sometimes be overcome by an encouraging teacher or a series of successful experiences.

An *overprotective* or indulgent atmosphere prevents a child from learning by denying him practice in coping with difficult situations. Efforts to protect him from unpleasantness, sadness, and the reality of situations prevent him from developing courage and self-reliance. An indulgent atmosphere often produces the "getter" lifestyle exhibited by the passive, dependent individual who is continually concerned with "What's in it for me?" [5] Another type fostered by an overprotective atmosphere is "the baby" who feels small, weak and helpless; he is unable to function independently but tries to put others in his service.[5] Sometimes this trait is considered acceptable in women, but this type of person often lacks self-confidence, has a strong need for approval, and exhibits a high degree of dependence.

The *pitying* atmosphere may surround a person who is handicapped, sickly, or has suffered a loss or misfortune. Feeling sorry for a child is disrespectful to him. Even pity justified by the situation is damaging because we encourage the child to feel sorry for himself, to be discouraged, and to expect special privileges. "Victims" who see life as abusive, full of suffering and tragedy are often the result of a pitying atmosphere.[5]

The family climate which espouses high expectations and goals is referred to as the *high standards* atmosphere. Contrary to common belief, high parental standards are often a hindrance to the child's development. When the child feels that he cannot live up to these standards, he becomes discouraged and feels inferior and inadequate, although he may be performing quite adequately by objective evaluations. Even when he is performing well and in accordance with the family's expectations, he worries too much about possible failure and overemphasizes the need for total success. Tenseness and signs of stress are commonly found. An atmosphere which combines high standards, competition, and overprotection frequently produces "controllers" who have the goal of perfection but cover up their true feelings.[5] These people need guidelines for everything and develop rituals to keep life at a distance.

The *materialistic* atmosphere values possessiveness, acquisition, and money; security is viewed in terms of what one owns and controls. Material things are given greater value than simple pleasures and warm human relationships. Children in such homes may be naive about simple pleasures, have difficulty in later life in managing a home on a modest income, and often are inexperienced in human relationships. Such individuals lack inner resources and creativity. If deprived of their possessions, they are distraught since they have little else to rely on. On the other hand, many of these young people rebel and become vehemently antimaterialistic, much to their parents' dismay. The widespread hippie movement encompasses many of them today. Some are fanatic idealists and many search desperately for what they feel was missing in their home atmosphere and early relationships.

When the family atmosphere stresses success and each member tries to outdo the other, it is typically *competitive*. Competition may be demonstrated in positive or negative ways. A child who cannot be "the best" in achievement or behavior may gain some satisfaction in being "the worst." Many parents and educators point out that we live in a highly competitive society and that, therefore, competition is a necessary experience in childhood. It is true that competition may act as a spur to a competent child, but competition may also foster anxiety, apprehension, and the tendency for a child to consider himself a complete failure unless he comes out on top. Competition does not encourage a discouraged child and may only emphasize the hopelessness of his situation. "Drivers" or "go getter" personalities usually come from homes where there is an atmosphere of competition.[5] If both parents are highly competitive, this spirit will characterize all of the relationships in that family.

In the *disparaging* atmosphere there is frequent criticism. Those who doubt their own worth may overestimate the value of others and feel that others, in turn, look down on them. One common way of dealing with such feelings of inferiority is to become extremely critical and to adopt a "holier than thou" attitude in an attempt to boost one's own status by making others appear worthless. Sometimes one child becomes the "scapegoat" for the whole family. The all-encompassing "problem" presented by this child's deviant behavior may then eclipse the misbehavior of other members of the family. In this case, the danger to the mental health of the child who tries to elevate himself by being especially "good" in contrast to his "bad" sibling is usually not recognized. (In Family Education Centers the "good" child is often considered by the counselor to be the greater problem, much to the dismay of the child and his parents.) Children who are the target of disparagement become deeply discouraged. If the child is active, a violent rebellion can be anticipated, for he usually acts on the faulty logic that only by hurting others can he find his place. If all members of the family are united in their disparagement of others who are "different," "outsiders," or "inferior," the disparaging atmosphere tends to produce cynical and critical pessimists who neither trust others nor themselves, lack good will, get little enjoyment from life, and find it difficult or impossible to form good human relationships.

Frequent bickering and quarrels characterize the *inharmonious* climate. In this atmosphere parents may use their children as weapons to serve their own ends. Usually discipline is inconsistent and varies with the moods of the parents, and there is a lack of order in the home. A child who sees his parents in frequent conflict develops the idea that power is important, and he may become the type of person who constantly strives for significance. Actually he feels insignificant and is upset if his authority is challenged. He tires to "get even," has little feeling for others and uses others for his own ends. Another type of personality resulting from an inharmonious atmosphere is the "person who craves excitement." [5] These people have fun breaking rules, flirting with danger, "making messes," leaving everything till the last moment, and confusing themselves and others.

Another dimension of the family atmosphere is *family values.* Any issue which is of importance to *both* parents, regardless of whether or not they agree, becomes a family value. Each child in the family must take a definite stand *for* or *against* this issue. One parent may feel that school is all important; the other may feel just as strongly that formal education is of little importance. In this family, *education* becomes a family value (as it would if both parents strongly agreed on the importance or lack of importance of education). All children in this family must take a definite stand either in favor of or in opposition to school. In a family where only one parent feels strongly about schooling, education might or might not be of importance to the children. If the child is conforming or cooperative, he usually adopts most of his parents' values as his own. If he has been treated with respect, he will feel free to explore alternate patterns without any compulsion to seize upon a different set of standards to make up for what he has found missing in his family relationships or in his own personality. If he is a rebellious child, he will probably rebel against the family values, usually without being aware of why he does so. In his deep discouragement and rebellion he chooses an area that is significant—one that hurts the family. Examples of these cases are well known: an immoral child of a clergyman, the delinquent child of a judge, the child of a college professor who becomes a dropout from school. Maladjusted behavior in adolescents and adults is often connected with the value orientation of their families.

REFERENCES

1. Adler, A.: *What Life Should Mean to You.* New York, Capricorn Books, 1958, pp. 12–13.
2. Dewey, Edith A.: Family climate. In *The Vital Years—From Birth to Seven.* Toronto, The Ontario Federation of Home & School Associations, 1969.

3. Dreikurs, R.: *Fundamentals of Adlerian Psychology.* Jamaica, B.W.I., Knox Educational Services, 1950, pp. 43–45.
4. Dreikurs, R.: *Psychology in the Classroom.* New York, Harper & Row, 1957, pp. 22–23.
5. Mosak, Harold H., and Shulman, B. H.: *Introductory Individual Psychology—A Syllabus,* rev. ed. Chicago, Alfred Adler Institute, 1967, p. 24.

7

BIRTH ORDER

Floy C. Pepper

A DIFFERENT APPROACH to understanding a child's behavior is through a study of the family birth order. Adler taught that the life-pattern of every child shows the imprint of his position in the family with its definite characteristics. He pointed out that upon this one fact, the child's place in the family constellation, much of his future attitude towards life depends.[1] Viewing the child's movement, we see the formation of alliances and opposing groups within the family. Each person uniquely approaches the social situation and his search for a place for himself. From this perspective, all disturbing behavior indicates the child's mistaken concept about himself within the group and, thereby, his mistaken approach to others. By eliciting the adolescent or adult client's order of birth and his reaction to it as a child, the therapist can understand his current problem and lifestyle more fully.

The relationship between the child's experiences within the family, especially the impact of the family upon his personality, and his experiences in the world outside the family is our concern. Family experiences are the most important determinants of the frame of reference through which a child perceives, interprets and evaluates the outside world. The knowledge, habits, and skills which he acquires in the home largely determine his capacity for dealing successfully with outside situations.

Personality and character traits are expressions of movement within the family group, in contrast to other assumptions which attribute primary significance to heredity, psychosexual development, general individual developmental principles, or environmental stimulations.

The concept of the birth order as a dynamic explanation sees child development not so much as the result of factors which converge on the child but as the result of his own interaction. He influences the group and the other members of the family as much as he is influenced by them; in some respects he may influence them even more because his own concept forces them to treat him as he expects to be treated. Each child, in his early relationships to other family members, establishes his own approach to others in an effort to gain a place in the group. All his strivings are directed towards a feeling of security, a feeling of belonging, a feeling that the difficulties of life will be overcome and that he will emerge safely and victoriously.

Human beings react differently to the same situation. No two children born into the same family grow up in an identical situation. The environments of the children within the same family may be different for several reasons:

1. With the birth of each child, the situation changes.
2. Parents are older and more experienced or more discouraged.
3. Parents may be more prosperous.
4. Parents may have moved to another neighborhood.
5. Because of divorce or death, there may be a step-parent.

Other factors which may affect the child's place within the family group are the presence of a sickly or crippled child, a child born just before or after the death of another, an only boy among girls, an only girl among boys, obvious physical characteristics, an older person living in the home. Further, as Dreikurs [2] maintains, children are sensitive to favoritism of the parents or to being compared with other children; they become misdirected in life by assuming that their siblings are preferred.

The *only child* has a decidedly difficult start in life, as he spends his entire childhood among persons who are bigger and more proficient. He may try to develop skills in areas that will gain adult approval or he may solicit adult sympathy by being shy, timid, or helpless. The only child may exhibit the following characteristics:

1. He may be a pampered child.
2. If the only child is a boy, he may have a mother complex. He may become convinced that he will be unable to be as strong and masculine as his father.
3. The only child enjoys his position as the center of interest.

4. He may be interested only in himself.
5. Sometimes the only child feels insecure because of the anxiety of his parents.
6. Usually the only child is taught to gain things not through his own effort but by depending on what others do for or to him.
7. He may succeed in having his own way by playing mother against father.
8. The only child may feel unfairly treated when his requests are not granted and refuse to cooperate.

The *first child* has a precarious position in life; being the oldest should entitle him to the favored spot, and it frequently does. However, he may become discouraged upon the birth of the second child, and refuse to accept responsibility. The first child may be characterized as follows:

1. He is an only child for a period of time and has, therefore, been the center of interest.
2. He must be first—in the sense of gaining and holding superiority over other children.
3. The first child becomes "dethroned" with the birth of the second child. Sometimes he feels unloved and neglected. He may strive to keep or to regain his mother's attention by positive deeds. If this fails, he may adopt a pattern of uselessness or become obnoxious. If his mother fights back, he may become a problem child.
4. The first child can develop a competent behavior pattern or become extremely discouraged.
5. He sometimes strives to protect and help others in his struggle to keep the upper hand.
6. The first child sometimes directs death wishes or expressions of hate toward the second child.

If the first child is a boy followed closely by a sister, their personal conflict may follow a pattern of sexual discord. Since girls develop faster than boys between the ages of one and seventeen, she may press closely on the heels of her brother. He may try to capitalize on the assumption that "boys will be boys" and, because of social preference, take advantage of his masculine role.

The *second child* has an uncomfortable position in life and may try to catch up with the child in front and feel as though he were under constant pressure. The situation of the second child may be described as follows:

1. He never has his parents undivided attention.
2. The second child always has in front of him another child who is more advanced.
3. The second child feels that the first child cannot be beaten and that his claim of equality is disputed.
4. The second child may act as if he were demonstrating he was in a race; hyperactivity and pushiness are often characteristic.
5. If the first child is successful, the second is likely to feel uncertain of himself and his abilities.
6. The second child is often the opposite of the first child. If the first child is dependable and "good," the second may become undependable and "bad."
7. The second child becomes a "squeezed" child whenever a third child is born.

The *youngest child* has a peculiar place in the family constellation. He may become a "speeder" because he is outdistanced initially and may ultimately become the most successful child. On the other hand, he may become discouraged and feel inferior because he feels the distance between himself and his older siblings cannot be bridged. He may exhibit the following traits:

1. The youngest child often behaves like an only child.
2. He may have things done for him, decisions made for him, and responsibility taken from him.
3. He is often spoiled by the family.
4. The youngest child often finds himself in an embarrassing position; he usually is the smallest and weakest child and, above all, he may not be taken seriously.
5. He may become the "boss" in the family.
6. The youngest child may attempt to excel in competition with his brothers and sisters or he may choose to evade a direct struggle for superiority.
7. He may retain the baby role and place others in his service.
8. The only child often allies with the first child, since they are both seeing themselves as different from the rest.

The *middle child of three* has an uncertain place in the family group and may feel neglected. He discovers that he has neither the privileges of the youngest child nor the rights of the oldest. The middle child may adopt the following pattern:

1. He may feel unloved and abused.
2. The middle child may hold the conviction that people are unfair to him.
3. He may be unable to find his place in the group.
4. The middle child may become extremely discouraged and prone to becoming a "problem child."

Children who come in *the middle of a large family* often develop stable characters and their conflict with other children tends to be less fierce. In other words, the large family generally exhibits less conflict and strife among the children.

Every brother and sister has some pleasant feelings and some unpleasant feelings about his siblings. Each is likely to have pleasant relations when he satisfies another's needs. Since each child feels differently toward each brother and sister, the relationship between any two of them is very special. Dreikurs [3] explains that competition among siblings is often expressed unwittingly through their personality differences. As one succeeds, the other may fail and vice versa. When the strong sibling takes over, the weaker may derive support through his passive role. Each, in a complimentary manner, feels secure with the other and fulfills compensatory goals.

If a number of years separate children, each child will have some of the characteristics of an only child. Perhaps there will be two "families," if one set of children is separated from the other by a number of years.

The development of an only girl among boys or of an only boy among girls may present problems. The only girl or the only boy tend to go to extremes in either a feminine or masculine direction. Both may feel somewhat isolated and may have mixed feelings about their sexual role. Whichever role seems to be the most advantageous will be the one adopted.

From the moment of birth the child acts, thinks, and feels in accordance with how he experiences or perceives his world, and the way in which he perceives his world is to him reality. What actually happens to an individual is not as important as how he interprets the situation. We must remember that it is not the position in the family sequence that is the decisive factor but how the child interprets this position.

REFERENCES

1. Adler, A.: *The Individual Psychology of Alfred Adler.* Edited by H. L. and Rowena R. Ansbacher. New York, Basic Books, 1956, pp. 376–383.
2. Dreikurs, R.: *The Challenge of Parenthood.* New York, Duell, Sloan and Pearce, 1948, pp. 160–161.
3. Dreikurs, R.. *Fundamentals of Adlerian Psychology.* Chicago, Alfred Adler Institute, 1950, pp. 37–42.

8

EARLY RECOLLECTIONS

Arthur G. Nikelly and Don Verger

THE USE OF early recollections (ER) is one of many projective techniques which may be employed to help assess the dynamics of an individual's personality. As is common with most projective techniques, its use constitutes an art almost as much as it does a science. What makes the use of early recollections unique among the projectives, however, is the fact that in terms of time and cost it is probably the most economical technique presently available to the psychologist. Its use can provide the clinician with a quick glance at the client's lifestyle. In addition, the use of early recollections stands out among the projectives as being the only one which is completely unstructured.

When properly used, ER's can give the therapist insight and depth into the client's purposes, and can be used for explaining the client to himself. What he selects and recalls from his childhood is related to the immediate situation. Even if the recollection is mainly fantasy or a fragment of his memory, it can still be used as a projective medium. ER's are to be related with the client's whole life situation, and interpreted by also taking into account other, objective, current facts about himself. His values and strivings, and his feelings and perceptions along with his ER's are eventually connected with his lifestyle. ER's assist in the understanding of the client's repetitive patterns of behaving, of the constancy and unity of his life and of his evaluation of himself and the world around him. The client is simply asked to: "Think as far back as you can and tell me your earliest memory from your childhood years."

An emphasis on "mother" or a particular sibling, on dangers, punishments, illnesses, the absence or presence of an important member of the family, the first visit to school, the feeling tone among persons mentioned in the ER's, interests in special tasks, the emphasis on pleasant or unpleasant experiences all express the client's basic lifestyle.[1] Besides giving hints on the client's private logic, self concept and life goals, bizarre and unusual ER's can reveal latent psychopathology not otherwise manifested in ordinary situations. Mosak[2] makes the distinction between a report and a recollection. The former pertains to a general condition of childhood or a vague collection of incidents, while the latter pertains to a single incident, or specific detail. In order to assure a recollection and not a report, the client is asked to close his eyes and visualize the scene which comes from thinking back as far as he can in order to recall his earliest and most significant experience in childhood.

The following case illustrates vividly how an ER can disclose the client's current pattern of behavior:

> A very dependent and clinging female complained of chronic depression and a sense of hopelessness, and experienced nervousness and headaches when around people. She expressed bitterness and sarcasm against those who did not show much interest in her and she felt unappreciated and unwanted. She blamed the world for being too insincere and selfish. She had no real close friends and was constantly preoccupied with her own academic success, while devaluating the accomplishments of her peers and pretending that she had no need for anyone. Her ER was as follows: "I remember not being invited to a birthday party in our neighborhood, so I went to the house myself and looked inside through the window and made faces at everybody and stuck out my tongue at them. At first they laughed and giggled, but then they ignored me; so I went home trying to force myself to look happy because I really felt lonely and hurt."

Fears of abandonment or of losing close contact with others may designate depression or anxiety. The need to be close with others, and lack of the positive feelings for them may signify a trend toward schizoid living. Morbid fears over possible loss of supporting members in the family may indicate helplessness and dependency. A skilled therapist can reconstruct the client's whole life plan and give it adequate interpretation, so that his own memories help him see why he has been behaving the way he does at the present. He may also nudge the client into giving his own interpretation to his ER's by saying, "What do you make of this memory?" The more frequent and persistent the theme in these recollections, the more his lifestyle is particularly strong in them. The same recollections in two different persons do not mean the same thing, as other facts in the client's current life are also taken into account before an interpretation is made. Dreams and daydreams are often interpreted in the same way as ER's.

ER's do not predict the client's behavior nor do they constitute a need, desire or wish to be or do something. They convey his convictions about himself and his current attitudes and reflect the static present. His present philosophy on life often mirrors his long-range goals. Dreams, on the other hand, reflect the current mood of the client and are apt to cover a shorter range of his experience. The main theme or pattern is to be interpreted in a manner similar with the TAT themes, or the figure drawings, and are not to be broken into separate fragments. Starting with hunches, individual themes are brought together and their unity and pattern spells out a message which describes his life plan. The client's recollection of events and experiences from his childhood are selective in his memory and reveal his basic outlook on life. He may produce as many as three recollections and the general pattern is interpreted from them.

The main purpose of the use of ER's is to discover the client's *present* fundamental view of life. Memories are psychological projections revealing the client's goals, attitudes, and style of living. ER's are not regarded as occurrences having traumatic effects on the client but as revealing the current outlook on life. Thus, a memory which resulted in unhappiness for the subject at the time of its alleged occurrence may be indicative of a general state of melancholy at the present. Before one can interpret an ER, it is necessary to obtain sufficient details of the recollection. It is not important to a therapist whether the client's early remembrances are distorted, correct, or whether they are actually fragments and factions of his memory. They serve as a reflection of his inner world, without being fully aware of what it means to him. The event or experience reported can be interpreted by the therapist to the client.

Although it is frequently possible to gain an understanding of the client's outlook on life from solely the content or theme of an ER, it is nonetheless a mistake to do so. The therapist should not rely on the ER per se, or attempt to interpret without the full cooperation of the client in the interpretative process. In addition, the client should be asked how he *felt* about the ER at the time it occurred. For example, a client related the following ER: "I was about three years old. I was sitting in a wagon, and my five-year-old cousin pushed the wagon into a stream of water, about three and a half feet deep." The number of possible interpretations of such an event is large. Before even a tentative guess should be attempted we would first have to know whether it is recalled as a frightful experience, or a humorous incident; viewed as a deliberate act on the part of the cousin, or merely an accidental occurrence. The point here is that the client's feelings and emotions associated with a given ER provide the main interpretative clue. In this particular case the client did not evoke much of any kind of emotion toward the event. Nonetheless, the counselor "guessed" that the client viewed the world as a dangerous place; and that he is life's innocent victim, contending with forces which overwhelm him (three-and-a-half-year-old versus five-year-old). In a calm voice, and without a trace of defensiveness, he replied that the description did not fit him, it simply did not ring a bell. His judgment was accepted as being correct and a second guess was proffered: "You feel that you are too helpless to do much on your behalf. Things simply happen to you through no fault of your own, and there is not much you can do about it." He smiled, "That fits me pretty well."

While the earliest recollection is often the *single* most useful recollection, it is not always so. Furthermore even in those cases where the earliest recollection is the one most helpful, the three earliest recollections, presented in the supposed chronological order, are frequently even more helpful. This is particularly true when it is difficult to understand any single ER, but a pattern emerges in two of the first three ER's. While the first three ER's may bear at least 75 per cent of the fruit, it is not without precedent that the first ten ER's are elicited. However, when ten ER's are obtained, it is necessary to try to ascertain the age of the client at the time of the alleged occurrence of each ER. Generally speaking, only those ER's which occur before the age of eight are likely to reflect the client's lifestyle. Should the recollection be too brief or unclear, the client can be asked to elaborate on it. Although generally all ER's convey a message regarding one's lifestyle, relatively simple and guileless recollections are apt to be more revealing and valid as compared to very vivid, emotionally stirring and colorful memories described with theatrical overtones.

There are occasions when a single ER may be of help in vocational guidance. Granted these occasions may be infrequent, it is sometimes these infrequent occasions when an ER is most useful. A highly intelligent girl could not decide whether to major in home economics or secretarial science. According to the counselor, the student had both interest and aptitude for secretarial work, and many other objective considerations pointed to this as an appropriate choice for a major. These considerations led both the student and her counselor to agree that secretarial science would be the appropriate choice. But there was one difficulty. The student wanted to major in home economics (which included dress design and construction) and did not know why. However, she was able to relate the following ER: "I remember my mother giving me my sister's hand-me-down clothes." This in turn reflected concern whether she was loved as much as her sister. The girl understood for the first time her "interest" in home economics and enrolled in the secretarial program.

While the client may not be able to understand his own recollections, it is often his response to initial interpretations which can either confirm or reject them, and can provide guidelines for subsequent, and hopefully, more accurate interpretations on the part of the therapist. There are, of course, occasions when the therapist may not deem it wise to share the interpretation with the client. In these cases the client's responses cannot be used as a check of the validity of the ER interpretation. There are occasions when a client is unwilling or unable to relate his ER. This usually means that, at least in the present moment, he is unwilling to reveal too much of himself to the therapist. This should serve as a warning that the therapist may be moving too fast. In addition, it may also suggest that the client is uncooperative and/or is not sure whether he really wishes to be helped. While the elicitation of more than one ER helps to provide a more complete and accurate picture of the client, subsequent ER's frequently cloud the picture because of apparent contradictions between the first and subsequent ER's. These apparent contradictions must be understood in their total context.

ER's will often change before and after therapy in the same way the client's attitudes about himself and toward life are altered after treatment or following an unusual phase in his life. The persons mentioned in the ER's may not necessarily be the actual ones involved in the client's life; for instance, "mother" may refer to sister, teacher, and female peers. Passive persons often recall observing others playing or working, while outgoing, active clients mention self-activity and initiative in their ER's. The mention of mother often suggests pampering. Physicians will recall sick people and accidents, while artists mention the color of clothes and scenery. Athletes often cite sports and games in their recollections, and those having academic problems are apt to remember difficulty with writing and reading. The same applies with religious concerns, marital conflicts, self-concept, etc. In addition, ER's can differentiate between subgroups of neurotic and schizophrenic patients.[3]

In summary, ER's provide a clear view into the client's current lifestyle, and they justify his approach and outlook on life at the time when he reports his ER.*

REFERENCES

1. Adler, A.: *The Individual Psychology of Alfred Adler.* Edited by H. L. and Rowena R. Ansbacher. New York, Basic Books, 1956, pp. 172–203.
2. Mosak, Harold H.: Early recollections as a projective technique. *J Project Techn,* 22:302–311, 1958.
3. Mosak, Harold H.: Early recollections: evaluation of recent research. *J Individ Psychol.,* 25:56–63, 1969.

* Mosak [2] provides many examples of ER's along with interpretations useful to a beginner in Adlerian diagnostic techniques, and in a recent paper he cites the diagnostic and predictive value of ER's based on research.[3]

9

PRIVATE LOGIC

Arthur G. Nikelly

THE TOTAL PICTURE of the client's personality may best be understood by penetrating into the depths of his thinking and uncovering his private logic which may be at the very source of his maladjustment. Normally, the course of this logic is neither immediately experienced by the client nor readily available in his consciousness and must
be explained and made conscious by the therapist. The client's whole
life plan and pattern of behavior is founded on his private logic. This
logic, therefore, is consistent with and illuminates his style of life in a
manner similar to early recollections or the family constellation. It is
within the private logic that the client forms his goals, and it is these
goals that explain his behavior rather than his "needs," "conditioning,"
or "emotions."

While common logic encompasses the similarity of values and the
validity of experiences and connects one person with another, private
logic is a "private map" by which the client makes his way through life.[2]
Since society, however, often will not tolerate grandiose self-conceptions
or beliefs which have personal rather than common usefulness, the
client, through therapy, must learn to understand his own image of the
world formed from childhood and alter those views on which his
maladaptive behavior is based. The client must become aware of his
subjective, biased view of life before he can be redirected toward har-
monizing his views with those shared by others.

The client's private logic is not based on a psychological cause-and-ef-
fect relationship, such as, resentment, frustration, drive-reduction, or

need-gratification. Rather, it is primarily dependent upon and consistent with his goals and intentions. The medical student and the teacher, for instance, are working in their respective fields not because of causative, antecedent events, but because they *want* to do what they are doing. Career choice depends upon the private interpretation of antecedent events and is not necessarily a direct result of such events. The client molds and reorganizes what he experiences, and the end result is predictable in terms of the consistency of his personality and is fully expressed through his style of life. The client is generally responsible for his decisions, even though they may often be based upon false or inconclusive perceptions of his experiences. Further, his convictions, self-appraisals, and secret intentions may create a faulty view of his environment of which he is not entirely aware.

To uncover this private logic, the therapist attempts to discover what the client tells himself when he behaves in a particular way. His reasoning may sound rational in this private dialogue but usually does not stand up to common logic. Once this private logic is shared with the therapist, it becomes less effective. The client begins to see how he gives up and bypasses the consensual demands of reality and manufactures his own logic as a rationalization for his behavior. Although carefully concealed, his private reasoning speaks through his actions. The aim of therapy, then, is to help the client see the consensual, common logic and the necessity for being bound up with the realities of living which are closer to his real needs than those provided by his private logic.

The therapist employs a *stochastic* method;[1] proceeding from fragmentary bits of information, he attempts to disclose the root of the client's behavior. The therapist may begin by asking the client to give his own reason for behaving in a particular manner. He may ask, concerning a specific action, "What goes through your mind?" The therapist tries to reconstruct what is going on in the client's mind during his maladaptive actions as well as during his report of them. Dreikurs stresses the dramatic effects of this technique for behavior change which he calls guessing the "hidden reason."[3] The client's hidden rationalizations eventually become apparent, and he begins to understand the therapist's explanations for his behavior. The therapist must be careful not to feed into the client's scheme and goals; rather, the therapist must expose these goals and then allow the client to decide how he wants to act. On the basis of clues from the client's history and early recollections, the therapist formulates a tentative hypothesis in order to see what reaction it receives. This reaction may vary from a fleeting facial expression to an undue emotional response. The therapist may even question directly, "Is it possible that you may . . . ?" or "I get the impression that you are doing this because. . . ." The following case illustrates how private logic may be disclosed through therapy.

A female student complained of depression and loneliness and of an inability to relate with men in a meaningful way for any length of time. At first she exhibited a cold and hostile appearance, but as therapy progressed, she became extremely emotional, dependent, and demanding. She explained that her role outside therapy was "masculine" compared to her role in therapy which was "feminine" and therefore less desirable. She described her father as "extremely masculine but a little child inside," as a man "who fought and dominated her mother and deprived her of her femininity." She had sided with her mother and had taken a hostile and competitive attitude toward her father. Her older male sibling by three years was never close to her. She admitted admiring masculine attitudes and characteristics such as independence, coldness, sarcasm, and intellectualism and enjoyed meeting and challenging men on this level. She would frankly have preferred to be a boy and consequently abhorred feminine traits in men, such as passivity, obsequity, and dependence which implied "weakness."

The student's earliest recollection involved "walking alone in the streets," and she reacted to this experience with feelings of depression. Her most frequent daydream concerned "being in the company of a 'cool' man who is always there to support me." She enjoyed playing the "cool and hippie role" herself, pretending that she did not need anyone. She also believed that "It's up to them to break the ice and come to get me, if they are really interested in me." In the meantime, she was concerned with society's "false values" and looked upon any kind of personal interaction as "playing games," even interpreting her therapist's genuine interest as a "game."

She had become sexually involved with a married man who had fallen short of her expectations, for he did not gratify her dependency and emotional needs. Consequently, she concluded that all men cannot measure up to her standards. She began to entertain fantasies of having men satisfy her sexual needs "any time I wish, because I just can't wait for them to decide when." On a few occasions she "cruised" alone looking for a physically handsome male but was instantly "turned off" from those she met, since they were not "on the same intellectual level."

In about the sixth session, the therapist was able to verbalize the pattern of private logic which her actions and account of them had disclosed. She stated, "I am all that a man wants from a woman, and I can make any man happy; I am a superior person who can give, but I won't give myself to anyone unless I am sure he will give me just as much or even more. The 'creeps' I meet are not bright enough to keep up with me, and they turn me off. I have the right to expect someone special for me, because I consider myself to be a special person." She became angry when the therapist confronted her with the invalidity of her self-styled superiority over men and with the purpose behind it. The student soon broke down in tears and acknowledged, "That's me" when her hitherto unverbalized private logic was revealed to her more directly approximately as follows: "Despite your superior intelligence and reasonable physical attractiveness, you obviously have an opinion of yourself which others do not share. You are protesting against your femininity by emulating while deprecating men and by competing with them in masculine ways. *You have formed the idea that femininity and moderate dependency are synonymous with weakness which you must constantly deny.* You are trying to stave off your dependency and feminine traits by maintaining an elevated and masculine image of yourself. Since this inadequate solution always fails, you react with depression and feelings of dejection. Your private logic clearly reveals the reasoning upon which your pattern of behavior is based."

As in the above example, the therapist must extract and interpret to the client his private reasoning, confirmed from the account of events surrounding the presenting problem. The client usually acknowledges the therapist's explanation with an emotional response, the "recognition reflex" which denotes apparent agreement with the therapist's interpretation.[4] It should be noted that in explaining the private logic to the client his goals are interpreted by the therapist rather than the causes of his behavior.

REFERENCES

1. Adler, A.: *Superiority and Social Interest.* Edited by H. L. and Rowena R. Ansbacher. Evanston, Ill., Northwestern University Press, 1964, p. 141.
2. Adler, A.: *The Individual Psychology of Alfred Adler.* Edited by H. L. and Rowena R. Ansbacher. New York, Basic Books, 1956, pp. 253–254.
3. Dreikurs, R.: The Holistic Approach: Two Points of a Line. In *Education, Guidance, Psychodynamics.* Chicago, Alfred Adler Institute, 1966, pp. 21–22.
4. Dreikurs, R.: *Psychology in the Classroom.* New York, Harper & Row, 1957, p. 47.

10

GOAL RECOGNITION

RAYMOND N. LOWE

THE CONCEPT OF goal-directed behavior, first postulated in psychology by Alfred Adler,[1] is rapidly taking a place along with other attempts to systematically explain the dynamics of human behavior. Dreikurs has made a major contribution to the clarification of Adler's ideas on goal-directed behavior in his presentation of the four goals of the child's disturbing behavior.[2] Although these techniques for behavior change of assessing and modifying goals are normally geared to children, they can also be applied to adult clients and particularly adolescents. Maladjustment in adults (personality disorders, marital conflicts, antisocial behavior) is often understood through their goals of which they are often unaware. In his striving for social significance, the discouraged person will engage in a variety of adaptive behaviors. Typically, these behaviors sooner or later become disturbing to others.

The purpose of this chapter is to provide some understanding of each of the four goals through illustrations characteristic of children and adults engaged in disturbing behavior. In addition, the reader is provided suggestions for proper corrective techniques which might be pursued once the goal has been determined.

The distinction between a disturbing child and a disturbed child must first be recognized. A disturbing child is one who 1) sizes up his relationship in terms of acceptance by those with whom he seeks a meaningful relationship; 2) decides he doesn't like the relationship and wants a better one; 3) seeks, usually through disturbing ways, to be accepted, and 4) runs into increased difficulty because his ways are

65

destructive, which further disturbs the relationship rather than improves it. Concomitant with his seeking to be accepted, he pursues short-range goals to gain "admission" to the group to which he seeks acceptance. It is these short-range, situational goals which are the topic of this chapter.

On the other hand, the disturbed child's goals are long-range, typically more serious in that the behavior is persistent, reflect more psychopathology, and are characterized by such terms as nervous disorders, psychosis, and sociopathic personality.

The counselor, therapist, or teacher cannot determine the goals toward which the child is striving simply by observing the child's behavior, important though this is. Additional information is required, and this usually includes some awareness on the part of the parent, teacher, or therapist about what his personal feelings are about what the child is doing. It also might include an observation of the interaction of the child with others and the behaviors engaged in by these "others" in response to the child's provocations. Finally, and this last is intended for use by counselors rather than parents, one might use some form of psychological disclosure in which the child's response to the counselor's revelation of the possibility of his purpose is used as a basis of deciding the particular goal toward which the child is striving. Psychological disclosure may also be used as part of the treatment or correction process in redirecting the child's efforts in being accepted.[2]

The *first* goal involves the use of attention-getting mechanisms (AGM). It is the most characteristic behavior engaged in by very young children when they feel they are not a useful member of the family or play group. Here the child seeks constant proof of his acceptance through mildly intensive but usually disturbing efforts.

Initially the child may seek approval or acceptance through activity coupled with nondisturbing methods. This is referred to as an *active-constructive* method of gaining the goal of attention. Commonly, the child's techniques are appreciated and he receives constant recognition for them. He may keep the adult busy merely acknowledging how helpful he has been in cooperating (e.g. "Mother loves you so much for being helpful" or "Here is some special treat for being so nice to sister"). The child will continue his active-constructive behaviors as long as he continues to get special attention for "how good he is."

One way of determining the accuracy of the diagnosis is to cease the praise and special recognition and note what happens. If the child was cooperating because he wanted to cooperate, when the praise is withdrawn, he will continue to cooperate. On the other hand, if he has been cooperating because he believes that in so doing he achieves special recognition, he may become fretful, anxious, annoying, or even obnoxious when the special recognition is not forthcoming (e.g. a child who works for good grades to gain attention will become quite upset when he receives a C instead of an A). The child who studies to learn may well be concerned but not alarmed.

Another way of determining the accuracy of the diagnosis is through psychological disclosure. When conferring with the child about his behavior, characteristically he is asked, "For what purpose do you think you like to please your mother (or father or teacher) so much?" Usually the child will respond by saying, "I don't know." This is followed by the counselor raising the possibility, thus: "Could it be that you like to hear your mother tell you how much better you are than sister?" or "Maybe it is because you feel special when your father tells you you've been a good boy today."

If the purpose is accurate and the child recognizes it through the act of disclosure, he will acknowledge it either verbally or through some bodily gesture such as a smile, a turning away of the head, or a giggle.

With the goal established, we are now confronted with the questions, "What are we going to do about it? How do we correct the situation?" On the assumption that the goal diagnosis is accurate, that of attention getting, active-constructive, corrective procedures should include ceasing to compare the behaviors of the "good" child with those of his sisters or brothers or acknowledging that the child has done well but not giving special privileges because of it. In short, recognize the child's growth in comparison with *his own* earlier performance, but do not compare him to anyone else or give him special recognition for his better performance.

Some children find they gain favorable position through inactivity or being *constructively passive*. These techniques are also appreciated and he receives constant approval for his positive passivity. Typically, his behavior is not viewed as maladjusted. The child gains approval by being particularly charming, by always doing what he is told, and by impressing adults with his seriousness and high sense of duty. Adult responses might be "I wish you could be as quiet as Susan" or "He never gives me any trouble—he's so quiet I don't even know he's around."

Here also the child continues these quiet behaviors or attention-getting mechanisms as long as he feels he is recognized as being someone special for being charming, quiet, or "good."

As in the case with active-constructive behavior at the attention-getting level, a verification of the child's goals of passive-constructive may be determined through ceasing the kind of recognition which has been given and noting if his response is one of discomfort, depression, or withdrawal. The notion of psychological disclosure is applicable here also.

The corrective procedures to be considered here are not unlike those suggested for active-constructive situations. The important difference, if any, is that the parent or teacher needs to be more alert in passive situations. Because the child involved in passive behavior is far more subtle than the one who is actively participating, the adult is more easily deceived into involvement.

Children tend to be consistently active or passive although seldom only one or the other. The child who seeks attention through active-constructive behavior and fails usually moves from constructive behaviors, those behaviors which are appreciated and rewarded, to *active-destructive* behavior through some form of mildly acting out. For example, Tommy seeks attention through constantly being a clown or showing off in class. On the other hand, Mary seeks the goal of attention through tattling on other children. These youngsters cooperate for a moment or two when asked to stop or sit down, but in a few minutes they are at it again. At the close of the day, the teacher or parent finds she is exhausted but does not know exactly why. Actually, she has spent much of her time being busy with Tommy or Mary.

In using the principle of psychological disclosure, the counselor asks, "For what purpose do you like to show off all the time?" or "Maybe it is because you like Mother to be fussing with you all the time." Here also, if the diagnosis is accurate, the child will in some manner acknowledge the purpose or goal.

Tommy, who disrupts the classroom by constantly seeking attention, might be given time each day to perform, at which time everyone including the teacher can enjoy him. The teacher must insist that while this is his time, he cannot expect to have any other. Instead of mother becoming irritated with Mary's tattling, she might ask Mary, "What do you want me to do about it?" or "I'm sure the children can take care of it."

The child who seeks attention through passive-constructive behavior and in his judgment fails, may move in a more socially unacceptable direction of *passive destruction*. Here the child tends to withdraw with the hope of having the adult or older sibling constantly prodding. He uses such techniques as being shy, bashful or late, excessive eating, stammering, laziness, and other displays of deficiencies.

The child always responds favorably to persistent correction but it lasts for only a short time. The adult, in retrospect, realizes he has spent much of the time trying to get the child to do whatever he, the teacher, has been trying to get him to do. Here also, as in the instance of active-destructive behavior, the principle of psychological disclosure applies.

It is important to remind ourselves again that the behavior *per se* gives us little or no indication as to the child's purpose for engaging in that behavior. Rather, it is in the process of verification that the determination is made. The child may engage in a given observable behavior for any of two, three, or even four goals. Verification is essential before intelligent correction can be undertaken.

Typically the adult prods the child. To correct the situation the parent must provide the information or make the request once and then follow through with whatever consequence is appropriate to the situation. All too frequently the adult designs some arbitrary punishment which bears no relationship to the situation and hence has no meaning for the child. For example, the logical consequence of a child being late for supper is not that he is reprimanded but rather that he misses out on his supper. When clothes or toys are left around, rather than fuss about them or continuously pick them up, the parent might serve notice that if the clothes are not picked up and put in the clothes hamper there will be no clean clothes when the child wants them. This decision should remain. With reference to forgotten toys, the parent might pick them up but the toys would not be subsequently available for some brief determined period of time; a day or two perhaps. In all instances, no lecturing or humiliation should accompany the adult's actions.

Finally, it should be noted that if a child receives attention only when he asks for it, he soon learns that if he is to be important, he has to ask for recognition to gain this importance. A more positive procedure would be to acknowledge the child's worth when he least expects it (e.g. when he is playing well, tell him how happy you are that he knows how to play with others).

The child who fails to succeed in gaining acceptance or his place in the group at the attention-getting level typically moves to a more intensive and disturbing level of relationships. The child ceases to simply seek attention but rather seeks to dominate, control, or be superior to others. This striving for power is the *second* goal. The form of correction suitable at the attention-getting level, although temporary relief may result, serves to intensify the misbehavior at the power level. Practically every opportunity is taken by the child to "put the adult down" in a power struggle. Seeking personal victories becomes a primary motivating factor in the child's daily activity. No amount of giving in will satiate the power-drunk child. An apparent victory on the part of the adult merely serves to stimulate the child to be more clever the next time.

The child who seeks to feel important through striving for superiority seems to be increasingly characteristic of children and youth of the present generation. *Active-destructive* behavior is manifested in argumentation which seeks to put the other person down, temper tantrums which result from not getting one's own way, seeking elective office in order to dominate others, engaging in sexual activity with no concern for the consequences, or telling lies to gain immediate advantages. All activity is channeled toward controlling others.

Typically, teacher and parents respond by trying to be more powerful in dominating the child and power struggle ensues. An interesting (although not too functional) test of power when it is suspected that the child is power-drunk is to ask him to do just the opposite of what you want him to do. If showing power is the goal, he will do the opposite of what you asked him. "John, you can't go to bed tonight!" or "You must use the car tonight because I will need it tomorrow night," when in fact you want the car tonight, are examples of this. Probably one of the most efficient ways of verifying the goals of an adolescent who is seeking the goal of power over you is your own feeling of being threatened. In this instance your own authority or position of superiority is being challenged. An interesting and highly effective method of verifying the suspicion that one may be a victim of power struggle through argumentation is, in the midst of an argument, to stop his contribution to the struggle and acknowledge: "Johnny, you know, you may be right!" The other party should, in some form, exclaim profound astonishment.

Psychological disclosure is appropriate here. One might say, "Johnny, you want to show Mother that you will go to bed when you want to!" or "You want to show Father that he can't stop you if you want to do it."

Positive corrective procedures involving the adolescent's striving for power are more difficult to manage than was the case in simple attention-getting. Parents and teachers who find themselves easy prey for the powerseeking child have as their first order of business to learn how not to fall into the adolescent's trap; or when they do, how to emancipate themselves from the power struggle.

One of the most effective ways available to an adult continuously caught in a power struggle is to simply acknowledge to the adolescent that he is more clever than you are by saying, "Johnny, I know I can't make you go to bed, but it would be helpful if you would" or, if the child is having a temper tantrum, "Johnny, I know you would like for me to get upset, but I haven't time right now." In all instances, the adult's acknowledgment should be neither punitive nor an expression of defeat.

An avenue toward improving relationships involving power struggles includes the adult's learning the efficacy of silence. Not to be upset when another person seeks to dominate you and to indicate this by not responding is to tell the other party that you are not interested in playing the power game.

Many parents fail to recognize the significance of *passive-destructive* behavior in striving for power. They fail to realize that stubbornness, disobedience, and forgetfulness are techniques frequently utilized in controlling others. They say, for example, "I don't know what to do with him, he won't do anything I ask him to!" or "He's so stubborn! Just like his father!"

The subtleties inherent in passive-destructive behavior at the power level are not unlike the subtleties inherent in any form of passive behavior at any level. The following techniques for verifying the goal of passive-destructive power are similar to those of active-destructive power: responding to the adolescent by trying to make him do what you want him to do; feeling threatened in the interaction; and ceasing to continue the conflict for the sake of observing the other's response.

There are at least three points in time in a conflict situation when a turn for the better can be initiated; before the fact, during the fact, or after the fact. One might possess sufficient wisdom to avoid the conflict in the first place. This is most difficult for many adults who appear to be possessed by the notion that they must prevail. With the conflict which ensues, one might catch himself and acknowledge to the child, "This is silly; we're not getting anywhere. I'm not going to fight about it any more." However, most of us feel that when we start something we have to finish it, and we still can do something about it after the open conflict is over. When the heat of both parties being stubborn has lessened, the father can approach the son saying, "Well, your old dad really botched it this morning, didn't he! But you be patient with him because he's trying to be less stubborn and with your help, he'll make it."

Typically, the child who fails to prove to himself that he is more powerful than his parents or teachers will resort to more vicious methods in *seeking revenge* for his failure to dominate. This is the *third* goal. Not only does the child seek to dominate, but he seeks vengeance in the process. What is most important here is to remember that even in these behaviors, the child thinks he will have some place for significance in the group. A child will knock over a goldfish bowl or break a window in the presence of his parents knowing full well he will be punished. For him it is more important that he be distinctive and acknowledged than to be ignored. His goal is that of hurting others; he gains some satisfaction in being disliked by others. He is the "best worst" in the class!

Adolescents pursuing the *active-destructive-revenge* goal provide the greatest single goal-seeking group for juvenile departments. Their behavior frequently defies understanding to the uninitiated. The behaviors in which this individual engages as he seeks his revenge may not be overtly different from those of the individual seeking power, (e.g. the child may lie, steal, cheat, have temper tantrums, argue, engage in illicit sexual activity, and the like. In addition, he may set fires, physically injure another, send threatening letters or make threatening phone calls). The determination as to whether the child is pursuing the goal of power or revenge must be verified before undertaking corrective measures.

Inasmuch as the child seeks to hurt those with whom he is interacting, a highly reliable basis for verification of the goal of revenge is your feeling of being hurt. Another method for determining this goal is to note the child's response to your efforts to encourage him. If his response indicates distrust of you or others who may want to help, it is fairly safe to assume the child is not only distrustful of others but is not trusting of himself and seeks unscrupulous means for justifying himself.

Because the revenge-seeking person is distrustful of both himself and others, most efforts for improving the relationship will be thwarted. All avenues toward assuring him that his behavior is not being "rewarded" must be pursued along with intensive effort to demonstrate that while he may hate himself, the teacher, parent, or juvenile court worker is not joining him in his self-defeating games. No positive experience is too small to exploit the notion that he is appreciated. A mere "Thank you" may be all the teacher can offer or an extended "Good morning, Tom," on the part of all teachers may be more kindness that Tom can resist. In such instances, the new relationship may be so strange for Tom that he may double his efforts to maintain the previous poor relationship. This should come as no surprise to the teacher or parent. Such behavior requires a doubled effort on the part of the adult.

Few children engage in the *passive-destructive*, revenge-seeking goal, but when they do, there is no mistaking the situation. The child's generally passive behavior is manifested in persistently expressing a negative attitude toward life, bedwetting, or receiving low achievement grades in school. These behaviors are accompanied by extreme feelings of exasperation on the part of the adult involved. All efforts at correction are met with expressions of negativism, such as "I can't help myself." "How can I help wetting the bed? I'm asleep." or "The teachers don't like me."

Skill in encouragement, both for the child and one's self is essential. Since every effort made is countered with an effort to defeat and hurt, the person trying to be helpful also has to be tough. The encouragement of colleagues has been a source of help to teachers who otherwise would have given up. The notion must prevail that "I know you are furious with me, but I'm not going to let you get me down!"

The child who feels so defeated that he has "no fight in him" will display a hopelessness and *assume a disability* about himself that is readily felt by others. This constitutes the *fourth* goal. His fear of failure is exceeded only by his fear of success. Both are sufficient to render him unable to function. He may arrive at this position about himself from any of the earlier passive levels. His efforts are feeble; he expects nothing of himself; he knows he is good for nothing. Typically he appears stupid, inept, uncoordinated, and he generally withdraws from all activity. It is at this level of functioning that the person ceases to feel inferior but in fact knows he is. He has acquired an inferiority complex. Efforts on the part of the parent or teacher to encourage him are met with a flat response or panic. The child either does nothing or displays a fear which quickly suggests that he ought to be left alone.

The person striving to find his place through an assumed disability is most difficult to move toward a more acceptable level of self-worth. Small gains and major losses are to be expected. Nevertheless, the teacher or counselor well versed in the behaviors of the defeated child will also appreciate the extended time and effort necessary to find small ways of encouraging him. When the child tears his paper when praised by the teacher, it should be assumed that since it was his paper, he had a right to tear it up. The child who won't try to jump over the vaulting horse in physical education, or sing in the group, or hit the ball will be told he does not have to if he does not want to and he can have another chance later on.

These series of analyses should not be interpreted as structured, mechanistic, and manipulative devices, but as positive suggestions and helpful alternatives. Principles discussed elsewhere are essential here as well, such as mutual respect on the part of the adult both for himself and the child, a sense of social democracy or social equality in which the child is encouraged to participate in determining those policies and practices for which he is held responsible, a genuine interest on the part of the adult toward the child, and the realization by the adult that he too is a mistake-making organism, and that without mistakes there is little or no growth possible.

Finally, the writer suggests that whatever corrective procedure is utilized, if the parent, teacher or therapist can conceive of an encouraging experience which will assist the child or adult in thinking that he will come out of the experience feeling better about himself than he did when he went into it, in all probability he will cooperate. On the other hand, if the child or adult, upon considering your idea, concludes that he will think less well of himself as a result of the experience, his attitudes will range from reluctance to total rejection of the experience.

REFERENCES

1. Adler, A.: *The Individual Psychology of Alfred Adler*. Edited by H. L. and Rowena R. Ansbacher. New York, Basic Books, 1956, pp. 87–100.
2. Dreikurs, R.: *Psychology In The Classroom*. New York, Harper & Row, 1968, pp. 27, 50–58.

11

LIFESTYLE

Harold H. Mosak

An individual's lifestyle (*Lebensstil*), his "style of acting, thinking and perceiving," constitutes a cognitive framework within which he selects the specific operations which enable him to cope with life tasks.[1] It expresses the central theme through which his behavior can be understood.[8] While he may not be completely aware of his lifestyle, he acts congruently within this apperceptive scheme, and we can deduce his lifestyle through observing his verbal and nonverbal behavior.[9] The lifestyle forms a unifying principle, a *gestalt*, to which behavior is bound in accordance with the individual "law of movement." Through this framework, developed early and remaining fairly constant throughout life, an individual interprets, controls, and predicts experience.[2]

Since the lifestyle is a subjective view of self in relationship to life, conclusions arrived at through "biased apperception" contain fictional elements. The individual, however, may persist in assuming that only under the conditions held in the lifestyle can he adequately cope with life tasks and find his place in life. When life puts him to the test, he frequently finds himself mistaken. He may then resort to behavior which he presumes will facilitate the evasion of life tasks, provide an excuse for that evasion, and protect his self-esteem. Both constructive and nonconstructive behavior can emanate from the lifestyle convictions,[6] and we cannot predict which behavior will coincide with a given lifestyle. We can speak only of more or less *probable* selections of behavior.

77

Probable behaviors associated with commonly observed lifestyles may be described as follows:

1. The "getter" exploits and manipulates life and others by actively or passively putting others into his service. He tends to view life as unfair for denying him that to which he feels entitled. He may employ charm, shyness, temper, or intimidation as methods of operation. He is insatiable in his getting.[7]

2. The "driver" is the man in motion. His overconscientiousness and his dedication to his goals rarely permit him to rest. He acts *as if* he wants to have "it" (whatever it may be) completed on the day he dies. Underneath he nurses a fear that he is "nothing," and his overt, overambitious behavior is counterphobic.

3. The "controller" is either a person who wishes to control life or one who wishes to ensure that life will not control him.[3] He generally dislikes surprises, controls his spontaneity, and hides his feelings since all of these may lessen his control. As substitutes he favors intellectualization, rightness, orderliness, and neatness. With his godlike striving for perfection, he depreciates others.

4. The person who needs to be right elevates himself over others whom he arranges to perceive as being wrong. He scrupulously avoids error. Should he be caught in error, he rationalizes that others are even more wrong then he. He treats right and wrong as if they were the only important issues in a situation and cannot tolerate ambiguity or an absence of guidelines.

5. The person who needs to be superior may refuse to enter a life arena where he will not be seen as the "center" or the "best." He may devote himself to socially nonconstructive endeavors—achieving the record for number of days of underground burial. If he cannot attain superiority through being first or best, he often settles for being last or worst.[4]

6. The person who needs to be liked feels required to please everyone all the time. Particularly sensitive to criticism, he feels crushed when he does not receive universal and constant approval. He trains himself to read other people carefully in order to discover what might please them and shifts from position to position in an attempt to please. He sees the evaluations of others as the yardsticks of his worth.

7. The person who needs to be "good" prefers to live by higher moral standard than his contemporaries. Sometimes these standards are higher than God's, since he acts as if God will forgive trespasses that he, himself, cannot. This goodness may serve as an instrument for moral superiority so that he may not only elevate himself over others but may actually discourage the "inferior" person, a frequent device of the "model child" [4] or the alcoholic's wife.

8. The person who opposes everything life demands or expects of him rarely possess a positive program in which he stands *for* something. He only knows he is against the wishes or policies of others. He may behave passively, not openly opposing but merely circumventing the demands of others. "Mother deafness" is not uncommon in children of this type.

9. Everything befalls the "victim," sometimes called the *schlimazel*.[3,10] Innocently or actively he pursues the vocation of "disaster chaser." Associated characteristics may be a feeling of nobility, self-pity, resignation, or proneness to accident. Secondarily, he may seek the sympathy or pity of others.

10. The "martyr" is, in some respects, similar to the "victim." The "martyr" also suffers, but whereas the "victim" merely "dies," the "martyr" dies for a cause or for principle. His goal is the attainment of nobility, and his vocation is that of "injustice collector." Some martyrs advertise their suffering to an unconcerned audience, thus accusing them of further injustice; others enhance their nobility by silently enduring and suffering.

11. The "baby" finds his place in life through charm, cuteness, and the exploitation of others. Often his voice is high pitched, and the intonation and meter of his speech is childlike. Often he has been the baby in his family constellation, but this is not a necessary condition.

12. The inadequate person acts as if he cannot do anything right. Through his default, he indentures others as his servants. He may be clumsy or awkward; he may limit his activities to those few where he is certain he will succeed; he may fail whenever responsibility is given him. Since his behavior proclaims his inferiority, he is the paradigm of the inferiority complex.

13. The person who avoids feelings may fear his own spontaneity

which might move him in directions for which he has not preplanned. He holds the conviction that man is a rational being and that reason can solve all problems. He lacks social presence and feels comfortable only in those situations where intellectual expression is prized. His most valued techniques are logic, rationalization, intellectualization, and "talking a good game."

14. The "excitement seeker" despises routine and repetitive activities, seeks novel experiences, and revels in commotion. When life becomes dull, he stimulates or provokes it in order to create excitement. He requires the presence of other people and often places himself in league with others on whom he can rely to assist him in search for excitement. Some excitement seekers, however, do not involve others and find excitement through fears, rumination, or masturbation.

Since the individual is holistic, his lifestyle may be assessed at any point—through either past or current behavior—and through a variety of behavioral manifestations, gestures, language, early recollections, or life narrative. Some Adlerians who do a formal analysis of a client's lifestyle collect information concerning his family constellation—birth order, sibling relationships, achievements and deficiencies, parent-child relationships, parental relationships, and family climate. To understand his current outlook and goals the client's early recollections are interpreted. The goal of this diagnostic activity is to elicit the *pattern* of living—the lifestyle.

REFERENCES

1. Adler, A.: *The Individual Psychology of Alfred Adler.* Edited by H. L. and Rowena R. Ansbacher. New York, Basic Books, 1956, pp. 172–202.
2. Ansbacher, H.: Lifestyle: A historical and systematic review. *J Individ Psychol,* 23:191–212, 1967.
3. Berne, E.: *Games People Play.* New York, Grove Press, 1964, pp. 113–114.
4. Dreikurs, R.: *The Challenge of Parenthood.* New York, Duell, Sloan and Pearce, 1948, pp. 187–281.
5. Mosak, H. H.: The Controller: A Social Interpretation of the Anal Character. H. H. Mosak (Ed.): *Alfred Adler Centennial Volume.* In press.
6. Mosak, H. H.: Early recollections as a projective technique. *J Project Techn,* 22:302–311, 1958.

7. Mosak, H. H.: The Getting Type: A parsimonious social interpretation of the oral character. *J Individ Psychol*, 15:193–196, 1959.

8. Mosak, H. H.: The Interrelatedness of the neuroses through central themes. *J Individ Psychol*, 24:67–70, 1968.

9. Mosak, H. H., and Gushurst, R.: What Patients Say and What They Mean. Unpublished.

10. Rosten, L.: *The Joys of Yiddish*. New York, McGraw Hill, 1968, pp. 347–348.

Part III   Basic Therapeutic Techniques

12

ACTION-ORIENTED METHODS

Arthur G. Nikelly and Walter E. O'Connell

THE GOAL OF PSYCHOTHERAPY is to help the client overcome avoidance behavior, to encourage him, to teach him outsight, and to instill social skills which he can practice without fear of being punished.[2] These skills must be practiced in social situations because it was in those situations that he learned his maladaptive and self-defeating responses. Often his therapeutic program can be worked out by a team of other clients or therapists which may encourage greater acceptance of criticism, help the client to face past and potential failure, and genuinely increase his feeling toward others. Further, as the client interacts with the group, the therapist can observe him in action and may understand his pattern of behavior, his lifestyle, more clearly and more quickly than through a more introspective method where anamnestic material may be baised and selective. While action-oriented therapy is designed for group settings, it can also be applied to individual therapy.

The psychotherapist must maintain an optimistic view of human behavior and be able to demonstrate social interest in the therapeutic situation. He should, of course, avoid psychological fatalism and refrain from espousing views which tend to dehumanize the individual and reduce the client's confidence.[3]

It is well known that distraught individuals tend to exhibit habitual responses toward their inner reactions and perpetuate their unpleasant experiences by responding to these inner reactions with negative attitudes. For instance, they may make unreasonable demands of others which are not or cannot be satisfied and then react in a negative defensive way because they fail to recognize that their demands were great or inappropriate for the situation. A similar view of psychopathology asserts that the problem of the maladjusted person involves an inability to exhibit responsible living. Consequently, he should not be punished or preached to but must be helped to recognize that because of the consequences of his behavior his present reactions must be modified. In other words, as the therapist instills an awareness of goal directiveness in the client, the latter understands how goals of which he may be largely unaware are often responsible for the way he acts at a given moment. In addition, the client must eventually learn to satisfy his own needs without interfering with those of others. He must be able to recognize and accept his own mistakes and to provide alternative responses if he is to adopt a positive solution to his problem.

Action therapy implies that both client and therapist are trying to work toward constructive attitudes and goals and toward positive social relationships and a sense of responsibility. Such therapy techniques have been deduced from Adlerian theory which stresses humanistic identification, freedom of choice, and the consequences of behavior. Action therapy is designed to help the client initiate alternative solutions to his problems rather than to describe or label his behavior within diagnostic rigidities. The client can become aware of his own efforts to maintain defeatism by conquering others with his symptoms and can understand how he places himself and others in situations where the client, who feels vicitimized, tries to entrap others.

A therapeutic atmosphere conducive to change cannot be fostered without sincerity and warmth, and cohesiveness between therapist and client is built on complete freedom of discussion. In this fashion, the defensive, binding method of fostering a "disease" can be avoided, and the client is less likely to learn to be a disheartened injustice collector. The role of the psychotherapist is that of an educator who views his client as a student who clings to his negative view of life and continues to react in nonadaptive and nonadjustive ways. Instead of classifying the client as an immature person or as one possessed by drives and frustrated needs, the therapist views him as a person who needs tutoring and guidance in order to develop authentic self-esteem. The client is seen as a person who needs spontaneous and cathartic expression, as a person who needs insight as well as outsight. He must learn the expectations and motives of those with whom he interacts so that he can respond appropriately, and hopefully, he begins to learn these lessons through the trust and the nonpunitive attitude of the therapist.

The therapist should emphasize the positive aspects of his client and minimize the negative ones. For instance, after the client has expressed unpleasant and disjunctive feelings about himself, the therapist can immediately state that he respects him and considers him to be a capable individual who can become successful within his own limits. In addition, the therapist can ask the client to state what good he has done during the day or week and what he would be capable of doing given the opportunity and encouragement. Surprisingly enough, many clients will react favorably to this attitude.

An effective and practical approach is to encourage the client to interpret his own behavior and then to consider alternative solutions which might prove effective. In other words, he is encouraged to search his life pattern and to suggest alternative behavior to reach his goals rather than to seek for deep and hidden drives. The therapist can sift out unacceptable or inappropriate explanations and help the client gain insight into those that are actually interwoven into his lifestyle. The client must understand how others see him and how to gain esteem from them before he can gain self-esteem. At the same time, the client must be given the freedom to remain a defeated victim if he refuses to practice outsight (e.g. "living" the other through role reversals and doubling).

Although emotional release and reflection on his feelings are therapeutic, the client often responds better if his difficult situation is enacted by therapists and other clients. Rather than being intrapsychic, the client becomes involved with problem-solving activity and discovers human commonalities. In other words, his interactions are analyzed not his subconscious psyche. The client can be asked to verbalize his idea of his role during the therapy session and the role he thinks the therapist should play. He can then be nudged into expressing the use and appropriateness of the roles of other persons or groups (peers, parents, etc.) as well as his own. Such probing often leads into insight and outsight, especially if the therapist can echo the role which the client is displaying so that the client can see how others view him. This *mirror* technique can also be achieved by having the client play the role of the therapist which serves to strengthen the client's feeling of empathy. The therapist can also verbalize the client's hidden feelings of defeat, triumph, suffering, egoism, by doubling, or by asking indirect questions that challenge the client's thoughts, such as, "Why haven't I ever thought of stealing?" in the case of an irresponsible, passive-aggressive person or "Why don't I consider a divorce?" when confronting a passive mate in therapy. This *doubling* technique may lead to a sharing of hidden premises about the world.

Humor can be effective in helping the client relate more positively toward the therapist. The client must begin to develop some kind of intellectual awareness in order to understand how much of his behavior is habitual and how much is more consciously created. Humor can help to disarm the client provided that the therapist is fair and honest with him and that the humor is built upon mutual respect and trust. Instead of analyzing and sympathizing with the client's dilemmas, the therapist deemphasizes these narrow concerns with humor. In this manner the client does not become guarded or defensive, and his behavior is less apt to become persistent and rigid. His tension is also relieved and often his hostility and aggression may be curtailed. The technique of overstatement, for example, may show the client that he is deciding (by avoiding anxiety and interaction) to see the world as a hostile jungle. "Let's see if we can make it even worse" exposes this maneuver and yet allows for an acceptance of the person.

The therapist may use the stroke-and-spit tactic. *Stroking* means that the therapist gives of his time and effort to help the client listen to himself and to cultivate an active, social interest. In *spitting* the therapist discloses the skillful maneuvers of the client, who may be seeking to avoid intimacy or who is directly hostile to others, and thereby exposes his ineffective ways of behaving (i.e. "Look what you are actually doing."). Spitting implies that the disclosure is unpleasant enough so that the client no longer desires to continue this behavior. Hostility from the client can be curtailed if he is shown how he would feel if someone else behaved in the same manner toward him. Responsibility, outsight, and self-disclosure are essential to the tactics of the therapist who utilizes the techniques of action or dynamic envelopment therapy.

The *Midas* technique ostensibly attempts to gratify the client's psychological demands. However, since giving in to his demands never solves his basic problems, he continues to remain unsatisfied and comes to understand that his fundamental outlook and style of living must be altered so that he will no longer rely on others for attention and gratification.

Another effective technique is *role reversal*. When the client makes unrealistic demands on others, he is asked to play the other person. By interacting in this role, he is forced to respond to his own demands and becomes aware of the needs of others.

In an indirect but therapeutically effective way the therapist can use self-disclosure to help the client understand why he experiences problems: "I would get depressed, too, if I wasn't interested in anyone." "I would be tense like you if I didn't prepare for final exams." "I would feel lonely and miserable, too, if I didn't have faith and trust in anyone." The therapist should demonstrate his own humanity so that the client understands that others, especially the therapist, also have problems. It is only the nature of our actions regarding tension and anxiety which separates the mature from the immature, and knowledge about these social actions can be learned. The dichotomy between normal and abnormal behavior can be minimized which will also serve to retard the development of dependency. When the client senses that the therapist is not omnipotent or free of conflict and problems, the client may become less self-punitive. He begins to see that there is something about himself which allows these problems to interfere with his life and that he may be reacting to them with exaggeration or undue concern.

Dreikurs [1] elaborated on Adler's technique of *anti-suggestion*, which is frequently helpful with obsessive-compulsive and "nervous" symptoms, by directing the client to practice exactly what he is making an effort against. Insomnia, finger-biting, hair-pulling, phobias, and other repetitive but unwanted acts may retreat with anti-suggestion. A premise underlying this technique is that such symptoms become aggravated when the client tries to fight them; as more tension is generated in this struggle, the symptoms persist. When the client is asked to intensify the unwanted symptom, the anxiety associated opposing it diminishes and the symptom is likely to dissipate. Although this method usually brings only temporary relief, it demonstrates to the client that he has the power to exert control over his behavior when he understands the basis on which his symptoms and personality operate.

Finally, having the client describe himself as he will be ten years from now, suggesting that he criticize the therapist, and requesting that he talk into an empty chair (which symbolizes frightening people) can be effective techniques in securing the client's active, responsive involvement. Another way to foster change in the client is for the therapist to serve as a person who is held up before the client for guidance. This will be presented in the next chapter.

REFERENCES

1. Dreikurs, R.: The technique of psychotherapy. *Chicago Med Sch Quart,* 5:4–7, 1944.
2. O'Connell, Walter E.: Psychotherapy for every Man: A look at action therapy. *J Exist,* 7(No. 25):85–91, 1966.
3. O'Connell, Walter E.: Humanizing vs. dehumanizing in somatotherapy and psychotherapy. *J Individ Psychol,* 22:49–55, 1966.

13

DEVELOPING SOCIAL FEELING IN PSYCHOTHERAPY

Arthur G. Nikelly

THE ESSENTIAL GOAL of psychotherapy was expressed by Adler with the term *Gemeinschaftsgefühl*, a term often translated as *social interest* or *social feeling* and implying cooperation, responsibility, belonging, empathy, and social cohesiveness.[2] Social interest may be considered a barometer for normality and adjustment and represents the striving for adaptation to reality which enhances the stability between man and his environment. Ideally, social interest is based on the desire to offer rather than to take and on a concern for the interests of the primary group and finally of all mankind. Adler maintained that social feeling is an inevitable condition for the achievement of personal and social harmony and will eventually become the most indispensable ingredient of mental health if mankind is to survive.[3] In the therapeutic setting social interest contributes to the development of feeling and attitudes in the client consistent with social reality. Just as the "ego" is strengthened through non-Adlerian therapy, social feeling is cultivated by the Adlerian approach as the client's behavior is met with an accepting and optimistic frame of mind. Theoretically, social feeling begins from childhood through the mother. In a sense, the therapist may take over where the mother left off, as social feeling is tacitly invoked in psychotherapy.

Social feeling cannot be taught but unfolds through activity and

The editor wishes to acknowledge the constructive criticisms of this chapter by Doctors Alfred Farau and Joseph Meiers.

91

communication between the client and the therapist. It is conveyed *first* through the therapist's verbal and nonverbal acceptance of the client for what he is without limitations; he is not at all obligated to please the therapist in order to be accepted by him. On the other hand, the therapist shows a continuous liking for the client while discouraging the development of transference which creates client-dependency and forces the therapist to assume a superior role which retards the development of social feeling in the client. An optimistic atmosphere is built in which the client is "won over"; he cannot help but *want* to change.

Socal feeling is fostered in a *second* way as the client interacts with another person who himself displays social feeling; in this sense, the client uses the therapist as a model. Social interest is a hopeful disposition and an optimistic attitude created from an encounter with another human being rather than the product of the client's insight into his personality dynamics. Social feeling is an "innate potentiality," [1] which remained dormant or underdeveloped in the client because of his mistaken attitudes toward and erroneous conclusions about his experiences. As social feeling develops, the client finds direction in his striving for significance—not by avoiding or going against others but by an active, emotional reciprocation. Through cooperative sharing he learns the pleasure of being constructive.

Social interest is developed in a *third* way as the therapist helps the client recognize his value as a human being or acknowledge, on the other hand, that other people (including the therapist) are as worthwhile and human as the client himself. Only when the client has developed self-esteem, when he can like himself, will he demonstrate social interest toward others and be capable of supporting his own existence. Such social interest is best communicated through the actions and attitudes of the therapist and is developed in the client as he witnesses and participates in the actual encounter of therapy. As the client confronts a person who demonstrates empathy, understanding, and openness, he eventually reciprocates. The therapist may suggest, "You have related very well with me, and I wonder how you would feel if you initiated this same experience with someone else outside our sessions. You have shown to me here that you are an authentic person capable of reaching out for others and establishing reciprocal ties with them." Thus, therapy becomes effective as the therapist demonstrates his own social feeling toward the client and provides the opportunity for a warm, human relationship.

Social interest may be activated in a *fourth* way; the therapist may openly and emphatically announce that, given the cognitive orientation, private values, interpretation of events, and goals of the client, the same problem or symptom would exist in the therapist. This acknowledgment by the therapist will arouse anticipation or at least curiosity in the client who now feels he is understood by the therapist. Social feeling has been kindled and may eventually be passed on to others. Confronting the client with his lack of social feeling may, on the other hand, only result in his agreeing with the therapist. The client may go even further and fabricate obstacles in order to keep himself at a distance and to place the initial responsibility for meaningful interactions on others. The obstacles are often expressed by a qualified "but" or "if" when alternate solutions are presented to him.[1] In this manner the client protects himself at the expense of maintaining a fictional superiority over others. The client may continue to manufacture reasons for being unable to demonstrate social interest because his private logic often equates cooperation and commitment with personal weakness or even foolishness. A crucial point in therapy may develop when the client wants to know "why" and "how" he is to implement a new approach to life through social feeling. By asking these questions he indicates that he does not yet understand the meaning of social experience and is resisting or testing the therapist. The therapist must help the client to understand how he is avoiding involvement. The client must be shown how he can overcome his real or imagined shortcomings, not through the use of detours such as using others, developing physical symptoms, or declining to participate in life, but through involvement and identification with the aims and aspirations of his fellow man. By subordinating his own needs to those of others, he eventually restores himself and becomes an effective participant in life. The client finds satisfaction and a place for himself not through seeking status over others, rather, by surrendering the wish for personal significance, he attains meaning for himself.

A *fifth* task of the therapist in fostering a sense of social feeling in the client is to nudge him into discovering a reasonable niche for himself, a place where he feels confident enough to relate with others without feeling that he will be the loser. The client can then allow himself to become dependent upon others insofar as he is willing to meet their dependency needs, and social feeling is nurtured as he receives in proportion to what he gives. The client begins to understand that he had divorced himself from others because of his doubts and low self-esteem, although he may have deceived himself into believing that he was independent of or superior to others. By behaving differently or presenting symptoms he placed himself in a category which resulted in his being treated differently; such a pattern reflects weak social feeling. Often the client may unwittingly maintain a polarized scheme by, on the one hand, adopting fantasies or unverbalized convictions that he is likeable, successful, and capable, while, on the other hand, perceiving himself as inadequate or blaming the environment or other persons for his problems. Either invalid position protects him from doing what he *should* be doing with his life and developing adequate social interest. The goal of therapy is to bring the client to a middle ground where distance and detachment, the opposite of social interest, are prevented, and tangible accomplishment, cooperation, and social usefulness are brought into play.

A *sixth* way for the therapist to develop social interest is to help the client become involved in concerns which lie outside his personal needs. He must become interested in the welfare of others and recognize their needs. By making his actions beneficial to others, he comes to *mean* something to them. Attitudes, values, and subjective reasoning begin to change as the client receives feedback on his behavior. He must initiate action before he can determine where he is making mistakes. In summary, social feeling and the awakening of personal significance are solidified when the client's actions have a positive effect upon others as they sense his usefulness to them. Another way to activate social feeling in the client is through the process of encouragement which is fully described in the next chapter.

In cases of chronic or severe alienation, Shulman [4] maintains that a primary task of the therapist is to help the client overcome his emotional isolation by providing him with experiences of social relatedness and participation. The more helpful the client becomes to others, the more he will be liked and appreciated by them. Tacitly but firmly the therapist must encourage conventional behavior by demonstrating to the client how others will perceive his actions. Autistic or selfish behavior must be thwarted by setting limits, if necessary. These techniques can be applied to severely withdrawn clients if the therapist assumes a more active role. A breakthrough often occurs when the client begins to see the relationship between his unconventional and self-centered behavior and the alienation and rejection that it elicits. He is encouraged to respond in alternative and more effective ways, despite his obvious failures. The therapist can point to the client's unsocial orientation to life and confront him with his self-centered intentions of which he is not always fully aware. The therapist must communicate at the client's level of comprehension and explore the client's basic beliefs and subjective way of thinking (his private logic). By demonstrating to the client that he understands the personal way of thinking which directs the client's behavior, the therapist often startles the client and makes his symptoms more uncomfortable for him.

Client resistance may be interpreted as a depreciation tendency which usually diminishes as therapy progresses. Negative transference, on the other hand, often denotes a sense of insecurity on the part of the client which can be resolved by encouraging him to assume more responsibility for his behavior. Positive transfer promises the client an easy and immediate satisfaction of unfulfilled desires. Adler [1] recommended that the client be neither spoiled nor slighted and saw in the phenomenon of positive transference the beginning of social interest.

REFERENCES

1. Adler, A.: *The Individual Psychology of Alfred Adler.* Edited by H. L. and Rowena R. Ansbacher. New York, Basic Books, 1956, pp. 134–135, 154–161, 343.
2. Ansbacher, H. L.: The concept of social interest. *J Individ Psychol,* 24:131–149, 1968.
3. Farau, A.: The Challenge of Social Feeling. In K. A. Adler and Danica Deutsch (Eds.): *Essays in Individual Psychology.* New York, Grove Press, 1959, pp. 8–16.
4. Shulman, B. H.: *Essays in Schizophrenia.* Baltimore, Williams and Wilkins, 1968, pp. 77–163.

14

THE PROCESS OF ENCOURAGEMENT

Arthur G. Nikelly and Don Dinkmeyer

Encouragement is generally considered to be basic to the therapeutic process regardless of orientation. It has been described as a common element in all major psychotherapies. However, encouragement of the client has often been neglected as a treatment technique, despite the fact that it is acknowledged to be a very powerful motivating and therapeutic device, for therapists have generally underestimated its potentiality as a means of changing behavior. Encouragement involves a kind of nonverbal attitude, which is transmitted to the client in an atmosphere of esteem and assurance of his worth and ability. In other words, encouragement is not given simply by making favorable verbal statements or by providing the client with ease of communication or greater freedom in his life. It implies that the client is provided with an experience of doing or creating something with his own strength and ability, and can be imbued with the feeling that he can deal with problems on his own. Encouragement is specifically utilized to assist the discouraged individual who feels inferior to others and has little confidence in himself and life. He typically cannot accept his humanity and its accompanying imperfections, and he is convinced it is useless to try. The less a person can tolerate stress in life the less courage he possesses, whereas, he has courage when he is socially committed and emotionally interdependent with other human beings. It is through encouragement that his tolerance for stress can be increased. Encouragement is one of the main procedures of the educator and psychotherapist for motivating the client to change.

Encouragement can be instilled by building a feeling of independence and adequacy in the client, and it can best be increased by having the client attempt tasks which he can achieve. This positive experience helps him to evaluate his attitudes and abilities realistically, and in turn he will be spurred into doing more things that are significant and important for himself. However, should he fail he can explore his mistakes with the therapist. Encouragement, then, is transmitted by helping the client to accept himself. In counseling this is done by really listening and intently catching both verbal and nonverbal cues. It is also relayed by *valuing the client as he is*, and it must begin with some kind of accomplishment, an act in which he finds fulfillment and satisfaction, which often changes the client's negative attitudes about himself and enables himself to feel confident to try again and feel appreciated for what he is.[1] The therapist's task is to help the client explore and become aware of his assets and strengths; then he helps him to activate his latent resources.

Encouragement is also demonstrated by developing a common goal and then recognizing even halting attempts to move toward the goal. The human relationship which treats the client as equal and able, worthy of respect, and meriting the confidence of the therapist is encouraging. By being provided with the opportunity to look at himself as others see him in the therapeutic setting, the client is able eventually to uncover who and what he is. This essentially is the first step toward an understanding of his actions and symptoms. He is not expected to change unless he feels *capable* and *willing* to change. The therapist is expected to communicate authentic trust and hope in the client's ability to change, provided it is reasonable and practical. A client in treatment for a long period, who had responded successfully to therapy, remarked: "I am amazed at your courage in having so much confidence in me." It was now *his* turn to demonstrate the courage by having confidence in himself.

In the final analysis the emphasis should be on the client's ability to establish his own limits, the model which he wants to achieve for himself and not the one set for him by society. This model, however, should be realistic and attainable. Finally, the fact that the client establishes a therapeutic relationship and rapport with the therapist is in itself encouraging, because he begins to understand that someone else is really taking an interest in him. If the client senses that he is *liked* and *understood* by the therapist, he eventually becomes encouraged to take an interest in others as he learns to be cooperative with the therapist; but before he cooperates he must have proper self-esteem and understand why he arrived at faulty conclusions regarding his personal worth. Such erroneous conclusions may be at the basis of his discouragement. It can be said freely that discouragement is an essential ingredient in all emotional maladjustment.

The goal of psychotherapy is not merely to develop insight in the client, but to encourage him to realize his own part in the development of his problem, along with the notion that it depends upon his own initiative to change his behavior, just as maladjustment is ultimately of his own creation. But before he sets himself out to redirect his private goals and reorient his activities toward useful aims, he must have the conviction that he can accomplish them. For the client to possess the strength and capacity alone to bring about a change is not enough, he needs to know the reason for and the results of change. He desires assurance that he will succeed if he tries, and he must regard himself as a person who will earn recognition for his efforts if they are motivated by the needs and expectations of his society. Above all, the client must feel that he will be respected for his efforts—even if they fail. It is the therapist who will develop an intellectual and emotional condition in which the feeling of encouragement will flourish.[2]

Clients will often claim they have no goals in life, that anything they tried has failed, and that no one would appreciate their goals if they had any. They feel that any goal is not worth pursuing because society as a whole is confused. This is a sign of deep discouragement which is treated by exploring the sources which cause them to feel discouraged. Apathy, lack of interest, depressive moods, lack of motivation, and a feeling of rootlessness may in themselves constitute a lifestyle which keeps the client on the defensive. By being alienated or disaffiliated he maintains *distance*. Distance is a convenient safeguard mechanism and a classical lifestyle for many clients who wish to remain apart from the world so as to allow them to feel omnipotent and independent. The therapist must see that in these clients such attitudes are simply devices for keeping themselves uninvolved. In the final analysis they are discouraged people because their misguided attempts to gain self-esteem and avoid anxiety have failed. The essence of the therapeutic approach is to make the client involved while showing an interest in changing something which is *within his reach,* so that he can gain more confidence and self-esteem and move on to further changes which do not curtail the freedom of others and are beneficial to himself. It can be seen, then, that encouragement is effective when the client is helped to make commitments to specific and attainable goals and comes to see himself as capable and confident.

Dreikurs [3] aptly points out that the technique of encouragement helps to convince the client that his problem does not reflect an inherited weakness or a personality deficiency; rather this technique suggests that his difficulty may stem from a faulty attitude toward life from biased premises about himself, or from the lack of social skills and techniques to solve life's problems. If the client can be helped to avoid seeing himself as deficient, he will be more likely to accept and act upon the possible solutions for his difficulties. Encouragement becomes effective when the therapist supports the client's accomplishments and performance, even his unsuccessful attempts, rather than when he praises his presumed but unused potential. It may simply mean that he lacks encouragement or that he espouses an inaccurate opinion of himself.

In therapy the client is shown the discrepancy between his unverbalized and often negative presumptions regarding his capabilities and his real ability to do what he can do *now.* He is induced to fulfill immediate obligations, no matter how trite they may seem at first, since problems and symptoms often signify a retreat from a real or an anticipated confrontation or from unpleasant tasks. Although the fulfillment of these tasks does not represent the final solution to his problem, the positive effort involved may eventually bring about a change in the client's self-image and outlook on life. Behavior change, then, is a by-product of the client's primary modification of his opinion of himself, of others, and of life in general. Furthermore, encouragement prompts the client to understand and to accept what cannot be changed while it tempts him to work at what is amenable to improvement. While he cannot become perfect, he can adjust his aims and become a less imperfect person. [4] Essentially, encouragement serves not only to acquaint the client with his lifestyle but to pave the way toward changing it—the fundamental goal of Adlerian therapy.

REFERENCES

1. Adler, A.: *The Individual Psychology of Alfred Adler.* Edited by H. L. and Rowena R. Ansbacher. New York, Basic Books, 1956, pp. 326–349.
2. Dinkmeyer, Don, and Dreikurs, R.: *Encouraging Children to Learn.* Englewood Cliffs, Prentice-Hall, 1963, pp. 45–56.
3. Dreikurs, R., *Fundamentals of Adlerian Psychology.* Chicago, Alfred Adler Institute, 1950, pp. 88–90.
4. Dreikurs, R., and Soltz, V.: *Children: The Challenge.* New York, Duell, Sloan and Pearce, 1967, pp. 36–56.

15

PSYCHOTHERAPY AS REORIENTATION AND READJUSTMENT

Arthur G. Nikelly and John A. Bostrom

ALFRED ADLER's approach in therapy was to reeducate and remotivate the client to become a more effective social participant capable of sustaining meaningful and rewarding interpersonal relationships.[1] He was convinced that dramatic change in behavior could be achieved in a short time by concentrating on the immediate interpersonal situation rather than on past experiences and childhood fixations. Adler eliminated the couch so that he and the client could face each other and foster a social relationship. Within the first or second interview, he would discuss with his client the goals of treatment and the approximate number of interviews necessary to achieve them. This innovation has increasing significance in today's clinics where problems often must be dealt with in a limited number of therapy hours.

Reorientation, or the working-through phase, marks the most significant stage of therapy and includes uncovering and interpretation of the client's personality dynamics. During this stage the client gains insight into his lifestyle, confronts his goals, and gains the conviction that he is capable of choice and decision.[2] The client must not be allowed to think of himself as the victim of past circumstances but must come to recognize that the problem is his alone and that he alone will solve it. In contrast, emphasis on past history may lead to rationalization and intellectualization without appropriate action. The client learns more and more about his problem and does less and less about it. The homosexual remains a homosexual, the schizoid remains schizoid, and

103

the suicidal client remains suicidal, content to count their woes and, according to their private logic, to feel ultimately that they have a peculiar advantage over others. A gross lack of motivation for change may be considered a symptom best alleviated without therapy. The client is told that at the present he is not exerting the energy needed for change and is invited to return when he is ready to make such a commitment. Such a procedure, when carried out firmly but with genuine warmth, often brings the client back motivated for therapy and ready to use the insight into his lifestyle as a *signal to act*. In summary, Adler's approach avoids irrelevant material and attempts to accomplish behavior change in a short period of time.

An initial step in reorientation is to establish with the client what it is he wants. Is he complaining about his environment or about himself? Are his wishes for change realistic? The therapist must be careful to discriminate between what the client wants from what he *says* he wants. If his wishes are unrealistic, the client may need help in tempering or changing these wishes. At any rate, early in therapy the client and therapist must reach a general agreement on the goals to be achieved, just as two dancers must cooperate to achieve harmony. Imagine the confusion if one performer danced the fox-trot and the other the waltz! To initiate behavior change after the client has recognized his basic life pattern, the therapist may suggest, "Is this the kind of person you want to be? Could you think of another, better way to act? What do you suspect will eventually happen if you continue this pattern for a long time?"

The client may stifle self-interest through poor interpersonal relationships. He becomes reoriented toward people and life situations as his feelings and perceptions about them become more objective and appropriate. Events and encounters and the relationship between them are identified so that the client can perceive them through common reasoning instead of through the distortions of his private logic. He must be shown the connection between his behavior and his intentions and goals, for he may unknowingly attribute personal failures to others or entertain unjustified wishes which can never materialize. Underevaluation of self, excessive self-interest, tenuous affiliation toward others, and erroneous interpretation of experience can be understood through analysis, and a more harmonious link between events and experiences gradually emerges. This process is also known as "reconciliation" therapy.[3]

The client is encouraged to work on his problem *now* by the therapist who must demonstrate that he is convinced that the client can change if he earnestly desires it. Should the client relax and assume a passive role or look for magical solutions, the therapist must tactfully object. The client's personality need not be unmade and allowed to regress before it can be remade; rather, the client can be shown steps for change which are reinforced through encouragement. The therapist may suggest, "Why don't you act in the interests of others and see how people react to you. Next time we can talk about that." Should the client hesitate, the therapist can motivate him to take steps by saying, "What would someone else with your problem do if he were in your particular situation?" Reorientation involves a kind of indirect nudging of the client rather than a directly stated program of action.

The therapist must understand that the client behaves according to his interpretation of what is meaningful and significant to him. The client learns or forgets whatever serves his purposes; however, such selectiveness may hamper his sense of social relatedness and inhibit self-realization. At this point the client may sense conflict and diffi-culties.

In our permissive age the client may experience little restraint against espousing unreasonable wishes or attempting to fulfill fictional objectives which must ultimately end in failure. He may complain of depression or anxiety because he feels he is not achieving what he thinks he should or because he is doing things of which he is ashamed. A student wants good grades but neglects his studies; a husband desires a happy married life but "can't resist" sexual involvement with other women. In these and a host of analogous situations, the therapist confronts the client by saying in essence: "No wonder you are feeling bad; you are doing things of which you don't approve." This absurd behavior keeps the client in a deadlock, and he feels estranged and frustrated. On the one hand, he wants to appear with "honest" intentions but, on the other, he seeks pleasure by using excuses and rationalizations. The client must recognize that relief will come only when he stops acting against his basic goals and philosophy of life.

The client must be treated not only on the basis of what he *actually* thinks of himself but also on the premise of the regard he *should* hold for himself. Change in behavior can be expected only after a reorientation of the client's image of himself which does not, however, destroy the core of his personal identity. It is not enough for the therapist to lessen symptoms or to develop insights in the client which make him feel and function better; rather, the client must become an individual functioning in his own right. Mere acceptance of the client by the therapist is not enough; emotional and intellectual understanding and dynamic involvement must exist between them.

Insights for and implications of behavior modification must be stated clearly and with respect for the client's freedom to navigate his own ship. If the client is not allowed to regress or become dependent on the therapist and if he understands that insight is only a prelude to action, he is apt to demonstrate a motivation for change, particularly if the therapist verbally expresses empathy and concern. Motivated clients often experience a "flight into health" after a few sessions, especially when their maladaptive lifestyles become vividly evident. Others experience growth more slowly, and the therapist may not necessarily travel with them on every step of this slow journey. Once such clients are convinced that the lifestyle has to change to accommodate a new perspective on life, they may want to "try their own wings" for a while.

Since constructive activity on the part of the client is a goal of therapy, the therapist must encourage assertiveness. Any type of inactivity in or outside the therapeutic situation should be interpreted to the client. Anything that is discussed in therapy should be interpreted to hold potential for action in life situations. Activity on the part of the client can be induced by the therapist in a nondirective fashion. He may need to provide the client with reasons and incentives for actions which are to his advantage. By urging the client to predict what will happen if he acts differently, the therapist may also encourage the client to take the initiative so that his actions may subsequently be approved of and reinforced by others. In other words, if the client acts differently toward others, they in turn treat him differently. Their reactions may spur him to alter his outlook and behavior pattern.

The therapist must understand that behavior is dependent upon attitudes which may have to change before behavior can be expected to change. The therapist cannot give to the client, but helps him achieve his own by taking into account all the factors involved with his problem. The client must learn to recognize the consequences of his behavior instead of relying on defense mechanisms to avoid such consequences. As the client experiences the results of his changed behavior, he is provided with a corrective and reinforcing experience.

The therapist should show the client how he creates and sustains his own maladjustment. Unattainable goals, for example, result in perpetual failure, and the client can transfer the blame to the environment which does not provide the opportunity to do what he wants. When shown by the therapist what he could accomplish if he gave himself a chance, such a client may set up difficult conditions which must be met before any action on his part can take place. To acquire a new outlook on life the client must acknowledge the necessity for change in his behavior, cooperate with the therapist and accept his interpretations, and feel fully accountable for his own actions within and outside therapy. Change takes place as the client understands his own behavior and becomes cognizant through encouragement that he possesses the power to implement his insights in life situations. The magnitude and level of this new direction must, of course, be appropriate and realistic for his case. As he perceives things differently, his actions change—processes which occur through the respectful and trusting relationship developed between client and therapist.

REFERENCES

1. Dreikurs, R.: Adlerian Psychotherapy. In F. Fromm-Reichmann and J. L. Moreno (Eds.): *Progress in Psychotherapy*. Vol. 1. New York, Grunne & Stratton, 1956, pp. 111–118.
2. Dreikurs, R.: The Adlerian Approach to Therapy. In M. I. Stein (Ed.): *Contemporary Psychotherapies*. Glencoe, The Free Press, 1961, pp. 80–94.
3. Way, L.: *Adler's Place in Psychology*. New York, Macmillan, 1950, p. 226.

Part IV   Group
           Techniques

16

GROUP PSYCHOTHERAPY

Raymond J. Corsini

Group psychotherapy has had multiple origins since a number of psychotherapists, independently, began working with clients in groups. One of these independent experimental innovators was Alfred Adler, who, in about 1921, began interviewing and counseling parents in front of groups of professional people. It appears that Adler's major purpose was to demonstrate his theory and his approach; however, an unexpected value of his method was changing the observers as well as the counselees. This method of open family counseling is the oldest method of group psychotherapy in current use.

In the more restricted sense of group psychotherapy as a formal procedure for dealing with problems of individuals via discussions under protected (i.e. confidential) circumstances, Adlerians, as true for other psychotherapists, have employed the group method. From one point of view, group psychotherapy is particularly appropriate for Adlerians in view of the social characteristics of the system of thought, and its primary emphasis on social interest as the ultimate concern of humanity. Putting this more simply, one of the basic therapeutic mechanisms that helps change people in group psychotherapy is *altruism* [2] and Adlerian psychology functions around this concept in contrast to some other schools of thought where the locus of attention is not on relationships but rather internal states.

There is no specific Adlerian method of group psychotherapy. What is generally held in common comes out of Adlerian theory, including such notions that behavior serves goals, that personality is formed by

111

interpretations of perceptions and by generalized successes in dealing with problems, that personality malfunctions are often due to basic errors, such as overemphasis on success in life, too great a need to be first, unwillingness to share, and so forth.

Methods of group psychotherapy have been subdivided into nine categories [1] and the Adlerian approach fits into the *directive-verbal-deep* box. This means that the therapist tends to be active, directing the procedure on the basis of his greater knowledge of human nature than the client; that verbal procedures are employed, that the emphasis is primarily on the intellect; and that an attempt is made not only to change surface behavior on a here-and-now basis by means of counseling, but also to operate in terms of insight. We should immediately indicate that Adlerian Family Counseling, the specific procedure developed by Adler himself, was *directive-verbal-superficial* and was counseling rather than psychotherapy, in the more restrictive meaning of the term.

What this means in action is that Adlerian Group Psychotherapy tends to be a therapy of confrontation. The therapist serves as a mirror reflecting back to his clients how they operate. Put somewhat crudely, the therapist "spits in the clients' soup" so that they can continue behaving as they have in the past, but will no longer enjoy doing this, since they are now aware of the purposes of their behavior. This element is most clearly seen in dealing with children. The counselor tries to find out what is the child's goal, a goal that is hidden to the child. He does this by asking the child questions such as "Do you do this (whatever behavior is causing distress to others) to get attention?" If the child shows a characteristic startled reaction, called "recognition reflex" by Dreikurs [3] we have in a sense spit in that child's soup in that from now on when he misbehaves he has insight into the reason for his behavior. From this point of view, Adlerian group psychotherapy is a Gestalt-type procedure, emphasizing the importance of insight by forcing the client to see himself as others see him. Shulman, for example,[4] uses the technique of exaggerating the individual's unique procedures for getting along in life to dramatically demonstrate what he does that causes him and others trouble.

Adlerian psychology may be also seen as a kind of religion, since implicit in it are ethical values. It is not enough that a person should become adjusted, whatever that means; it is important that he become adjusted through living a useful rather than a useless life. Consequently, group psychotherapy involves a changing of values, a moving of the individual from egoism to altruism. This change is not directed by preaching *per se*, but rather via the Adlerian therapist's deep conviction that only by democratic sharing and acceptance of one's self as part of the whole of humanity can the individual find himself. He must "find his place in society" to use Adlerian language.

The Adlerian psychotherapist always keeps in mind that man has three major areas of concern: *family, work,* and *society,* and realizes that all three areas are affected simultaneously by changing the individual's mistaken ideas about himself and society. To do this calls for 1) diagnosis and 2) correction. In this sense, Adlerian psychology follows the classical medical model. Diagnostic procedures, however, are of two types, and they often occur at the same time. They may 1) be of the formal type, involving analysis of family constellations and of early recollections, etc. or 2) may be informal in that the insights about the client come from observing his behavior within the therapy group. Consequently, the Adlerian therapist operates within a rather narrowly circumscribed frame of reference, thinking more or less in the following manner: "This person has developed certain characteristic ways of dealing with life (lifestyle) which he will demonstrate within the group, especially in crisis situations, and I must be aware of them; he has the task of getting along in life with society, with his family and with employers and fellow employees, and I must try to find out how he operates; he has some hidden goals, of which he is not aware, and I must try to understand them. But all of these depend on my understanding of fundamental errors he is making. He has some covert ideas which cause him trouble, and if I can find them, and let him see them, then he will gain insight into himself and be able to change his thinking and his behavior."

Note that in Adlerian thinking that feelings and emotions play only a small part. Adlerians see these as "sideshows" or as secondary elements, not primary. Tears and temper tantrums are only devices, or accessory phenomena, accompanying but not causing behavior. We see them as methods of energizing individuals, or procedures for cowing others, and so on, and in general we ignore feelings as unimportant. That is to say, Adlerian psychotherapy, group and individual, is essentially cognitive. We see a little man in the brain, directing behavior, and pulling the cord that signals emotions, but we do not view emotions as particularly important as causes of misbehavior. So, we do not say that a person misbehaved because he was upset; but rather he got upset in order to misbehave. As can be seen, the direction is from the intellect to the emotion to the behavior. First was the cognition, then the emotion, then the behavior. For this reason, all feelings and other emotions play a very small part in Adlerian thinking, and most Adlerians do not waste their time consoling people, feeling sorry for them, or being affected by displays of temper. The individual is always seen as goal-oriented, whether or not he is aware of this himself, and as using his behavior and his feelings for his own purposes.

In a sense, there is no Adlerian group psychotherapy, there is only Adlerian therapy, held with one client (individual therapy) or with several clients (group therapy). The constant factor is Adlerian theory and philosophy, as interpreted and as used variously by therapists. In contrast to nondirective counseling with its emphasis on feelings or psychodrama with its emphasis on action, Adlerian group therapy emphasizes cognition. Putting it simply, "a man is how he thinketh." The Adlerian wants to find out how a client thinks and tries to help him think better, and once this occurs, believes that feeling and behavior will take care of themselves. Both behavior and feelings may be dealt with, however, in such manners as pointing out that expressions of feelings have a goal ("You are crying in order to get me to stop asking you questions") or by demanding that behavior be changed ("If you want to improve, you must stop this nonsense immediately"). However, the change mechanism is primarily via understanding and insight. ("It looks as though you don't talk in the group in order to bring attention to yourself." "You don't participate in discussions because you feel that you can't engage in competition and want everyone to just listen to you." "You are always first in everything, feeling that you cannot share with others.")

In view of this, Adlerian therapy tends to be intermediate in length to the action therapies, such as psychodrama and the feeling therapies such as psychoanalysis. The action therapies tend to be immediate in their action, while the feeling therapies tend to be interminable. Adlerians tend to be quite eclectic relative to individual and group therapy; so a client may be in both forms simultaneously, or he may start individually and proceed eventually to a group.

REFERENCES

1. Corsini, R. J.: *Methods of Group Psychotherapy.* New York, McGraw-Hill, 1957.
2. Corsini, R. J., and Rosenberg, B.: Mechanisms of group psychotherapy. *J Abnorm Psychol,* 51:406–411, 1955.
3. Dreikurs, R.: The four goals of children's misbehavior. *Nervous Child,* 6:3–11, 1947.
4. Shulman, B. H.: Group psychotherapy in a post stockade. *J Soc Ther,* 3:14–18, 1957.

17

FAMILY COUNSELING *

BINA ROSENBERG

IN THE 1920's Alfred Adler began the technique of interviewing
school children and adolescents together with their parents and
siblings before an audience of teachers, mental health workers, and
interested parents.[1] He had intended to provide an opportunity to train
teachers and counselors in interviewing techniques, but discovered that
both observers and participants learned a great deal about themselves
and the dynamics of human interaction within the family through these
sessions. Adler theorized that since personal problems ultimately emanate from social interaction, such problems could better be resolved
with group methods than by treating the offspring in isolation and
returning him to the family in which the conflict exists.[2] Thus was the
technique of family counseling born. The basic premises regarding this
technique are that the counselor helps the parents to develop new
attitudes toward their offspring through understanding family dynamics
and helps the child more fully to understand his goals.[3] In line with
Adler's tradition, family counseling today is usually conducted in the
presence of an audience of parents and teachers.

As in all counseling interviews, the art of listening is of utmost
importance. In stating their problems, the parents reveal personality
trends which aid the counselor in making a diagnostic impression of the
parents and of the interrelations within the family. The presence of the

* An earlier version of this chapter appeared in Dreikurs, R.; Corsini, R.;
Lowe, R., and Sonstegard, M. (Eds.): Adlerian Family Counseling. Eugene, Ore.,
University of Oregon Press, 1959, pp. 33–40.

father is highly desirable, at least for the initial sessions. In observing the interactions between parents, the counselor can recognize the dominant parent—often the parent who speaks up first! As the counselor listens and observes, he must judge if either parent is too concerned with ambition, prestige, or discipline. Is either parent overprotective, demanding, or unsure of himself?

After the parents state their overall problems, the counselor usually attempts to obtain further general information. Typical questions at this stage are: "What do you think is the reason for this behavior?" "What have you been advised to do and by whom?" "What do you think is the right way to handle this problem?" "What have you actually done to correct this problem?" "What success have you had?" The parents should be given every opportunity to express themselves, should be encouraged to go on, and should be made to feel that they are listened to with understanding. Other members in the group should be helped to avoid premature and hasty judgments.

After perhaps five or ten minutes of this exploratory dialogue, the counselor should ask the mother to describe a typical day in her life. This portion of the interview should be structured to bring out her relationship with the children and the relationships among the children, with particular emphasis on the so-called problem child or children. "Tell me how the children get up in the morning." "Are there any problems about dressing?" "How does breakfast go?" "How is going to school in the morning accomplished?" "What do you know about their school behavior?" "How about playing with other children?" "Are there any difficulties in eating?" "How do the children get along with each other?" "Does television create any problems?" "Are there any difficulties with supper?" "How about going to bed, cleaning teeth, taking baths?"

When problems are mentioned during the family routine interview, the counselor should ask, "And what do you do about it?" The counselor remains noncommittal, if the answer indicates improper handling of the problem. For example, "What do you do when Peter does not go to bed when you tell him to?" "I tell him that he has to go, and then, if he doesn't after a reasonable interval, I take him by the ear and bring him into the bathroom. I wash his face, call him a baby, and undress him myself and put him to bed." The counselor may think that this is a poor method of disciplining a ten-year-old boy but at this point says nothing.

This preliminary discussion is diagnostic, but peculiarly enough, even when the counselor says nothing, the parents may offer: "I can see that it is wrong, but I don't know what else to do." Parents in the audience may be surprised to learn how poorly these parents do or how similar their own methods are to the methods of the parents being interviewed.

The counselor now begins to put the situation into context. He may feel that the mother is falling for the tricks of a child who is looking for recognition and demanding too much attention. He may tentatively decide that the child and parent are engaged in a power-contest, that the parent is a slave of the child, or that the parents' high standards are demoralizing and discouraging to the child. In short, a tentative diagnosis is made. Recommendations, however, must depend on an accurate diagnosis, and in spite of precautions, a counselor may misconstrue the situation. The wise and particularly the inexperienced counselor will keep his opinions to himself at this point and concern himself with obtaining further information. If the counselor has an hypothesis, additional information will help to confirm its validity and will help all concerned to feel more certain of the final diagnosis and suggestions.

This first part of the session is most important. Questions are raised but not answered. The counselor's skillful and persistent questions and understanding attitude serve as a model of behavior in such situations. What kinds of ideas go through the mind of the counselor at this point? Here is a sample:

> These parents are convinced that they have the duty to transmit their moral and social values to their children, but this may have led to excessive talking. The children may well be sullen and resentful. There is probably too much ordering around in this family, and the children may be reacting negatively.

> These parents have unachievably high standards and make their children feel inadequate, small, and inferior. These children have probably found that they can never satisfy their parents and are completely discouraged.

At this point the counselor must impress upon the parents that the basis for improvement in the domestic situation depends on a good relationship with their children. Such a relationship can be achieved if the parents learn to understand their children—their intentions, attitudes, and feelings. Parents are told that there are no bad children but that there are unhappy, determined, discouraged, or misguided children who have learned useless ways of operating in life. Dreikurs' dictum that a child needs encouragement the way a plant needs water may be emphasized. The counselor must indicate as generally and as kindly as possible that parents, often with good intentions and with the best interests of their children at heart, may make and intensify errors and consequently discourage their children. However, no matter what errors have been made in the past, conditions can be improved. Pertinent examples will help to illustrate this point: "Helping a child with homework not only gives him special service but implies that he is unable to do the work himself. On the other hand, letting him do it by himself and praising him for what he is able to do builds up his courage and self-respect."

The parents are then asked to leave the room, and the receptionist or social worker goes to the playroom to get the children. During this period, the counselor, imitating Adler, may make a predictive comment to the group about the children's behavior, may ask the group to be alert for typical kinds of behavior that the children may demonstrate. Some children come forward, shake hands, smile and talk freely about their parents and life in general. Others are sullen and refuse to participate at all. Both types of behavior serve the counselor's purpose, since he considers all the manifest behaviors as they relate to the nature of the family problem.

The counselor may put the children at ease by asking general questions which indicate interest in the child and his problems. These preliminaries should be short, for children like a direct approach: "What is your name?" "How are things going at home?" "Do you know why you are here?" If a child does not appear to understand why he is present at the session, the counselor should provide an explanation.

During a first interview, children may give short answers. As far as they are concerned, there may be no problem. Children are usually verbal optimists. The counselor is, however, interested in the child's concept of himself. Typical initial questions may be "Are you a big girl or a little girl?" "Are you good or are you bad?" "Why does your mother bring you to this place?" "What do you want to become?" "Who are your friends?" "What do you like to do?" The child's goals are interpreted to him by the counselor in the form of a question: "Could it be that you refuse to dress yourself, to eat, or to go to bed because you want mother to help you? Are you trying to boss her?" The child may show a "recognition reflex" by contracting his facial muscles in an involuntary smile.

After the child has been interviewed, the parents are called back. In their presence, the counselor asks the playroom worker to report her observation of the children, how they related to each other and to the group. This information supplements the information obtained by the counselor from the social worker, from the parents, and from the child. Reports are also received from others who have a responsible relationship to the child—a teacher, a juvenile worker, a social worker, a settlement house worker.

Now comes the period when the parents are given explanations of the dynamics of the child's behavior and when specific recommendations are made. Generally, the counselor is concerned with handling only one aspect of the child's behavior, usually the problem considered most pressing by the mother. The number of interpretations and suggestions should be limited, since if too many new ideas are given, the mother may become confused and discouraged and make no effort to change at all.

The counselor should be sensitive to the parents' feelings as he phrases comments. Generally, negative instructions should be given first (what to avoid) followed by positive instruction (what to do). The mother must stop what she is doing wrong before she can begin to do what should be done. "It seems to me you make a number of errors in dealing with your child; maybe you could stop talking and scolding so much." Among the usual suggestions are to stop nagging, complaining, threatening and punishing, to stop promising and bribing, to stop preaching and comparing, and to stop discouraging the child. These suggestions may be summarized by the simple and crude statement: "Keep your mouth shut!" These "don'ts" should be illustrated with concrete examples so that the mother firmly grasps what she must avoid doing.

After making these suggestions, the counselor asks the parents and the group for their opinions. It is essential to start a lively discussion. Often parents who were not counseled at that particular session but who are participating members of the group can recognize the errors of the other parents. Frequently, parents counseled at previous sessions will reinforce the counselor's suggestions as they report their own experiences. It is important that parents not only give lip service to the counselor's suggestions but that they understand why preaching, nagging, and threatening must be stopped. If parents ask questions about these suggestions or object to them, the counselor can offer further explanations or ask the parents to accept the suggestions as working hypotheses, to apply them, and to judge later how they are working.

The counselor then states: "I have told you what *not* to do; now I want to tell you what you should do. There are a number of problems, but let us handle only one of them now. Next time we can determine how successful you have been. If things go well, we can discuss other problems." While some general instructions can be given, oversimplified "cookbook" suggestions must be avoided. Each suggestion depends on an understanding of the dynamics of the children's goals. Quite different instructions may be given for similar problems if the personalities of the participants differ sharply or if the situations are not comparable. Nevertheless, typical advice can be presented by way of illustration:

You say your children fight and drive you wild, that they may even hurt each other. It is important that you don't interfere with their fighting. If you cannot stand the noise, go into another room and come back when they are through. If you can't stand the noise even then, or if they damage the furniture, tell them they must fight outside of the house. Send them out, telling them to come back when they are ready to act like decent human beings.

Your son is not doing well in school. The teachers ask you to help him. I suggest just the opposite. School is your son's problem, not yours, and you should not help him. Tell him and his teachers that you will not help him. If he fails, that is his business. Let him suffer the logical consequences of his behavior.

It has done you and your children no good to fight every night about going to bed. Tell them tonight that since they are smart and know when they should go to bed you are quite willing to leave their bedtime up to them. Let them go to bed whenever they want to but don't let them watch television or amuse themselves after bedtime.

These typical suggestions usually strike parents with horror and seem to go counter to all their ideas about child-rearing. Parents generally feel that if they follow these suggestions their power will be lessened. Again, a full discussion and explanation must take place, and the other parents are invited to participate. Frequently, the unconvinced parent will agree to the new procedure on a trial basis. The counselor may wish to add, "I am telling you what may be of help. On the basis of my experience I think these suggestions will work. You have to have confidence in me and in yourself to try out these new ways of proceeding."

Frequently, especially after the first session, the counselor tries to explain to parents the nature of the goals and demands that children have. All children need attention and love which is free and voluntarily given by parents; attention and love must not be won by the child through force or other improper strategies. Children need to feel that they belong in the family and that they have a respected place.

In the follow-up interview the counselor usually asks the mother what she learned in the first interview and what she did to deal with her problems. The counselor then reviews the previous session from the recorder's report and may check, point by point, to see whether the specific recommendations were followed. Generally, the mother who was able to follow directions reports partial improvement. Usually, however, she states that the experience was difficult and that the children took advantage of the new situation and were resistant. Nevertheless, mothers who were able to follow advice usually feel encouraged. They begin to feel strength in handling problems and realize that the advice of the counselor was sound. They begin to benefit from listening to the advice given by and to other parents. Sometimes dramatic changes are reported in the children's behavior and the tenor of the family seems to have improved. On the other hand, some mothers are unable to follow recommendations. The counselor must give such a mother confidence in herself so that she will be able to put new methods into effect, regardless of the disapproving attitudes of family and friends. Other mothers can be of great help to her since she will feel supported by the group and gain confidence as she hears the dramatic testimonials of other mothers. In cases where parents remain unable to follow directions, referrals for psychotherapy may be necessary.

REFERENCES

1. Adler, A.: *The Individual Psychology of Alfred Adler.* Edited by H. L. and Rowena R. Ansbacher. New York, Basic Books, 1956, pp. 392–398.
2. Adler, A.: *Superiority and Social Interest.* Edited by H. L. and Rowena R. Ansbacher. Evanston, Ill., Northwestern University Press, 1964, pp. 374–382.
3. Dreikurs, R.: *The Challenge of Parenthood.* New York, Duell, Sloan & Pearce, 1948, pp. 187–281.

18

MARITAL THERAPY

Wilmer L. Pew and Miriam L. Pew

THE UNIQUE FORM of marital therapy described in this chapter is derived from Adlerian teleoanalysis and group and multiple therapy.[3] It involves the concurrent treatment of a couple by two therapists who are married to each other. At the beginning of the first session each spouse is asked to describe the presenting problem as he sees it, with little emphasis on detailed past history. When only one spouse seeks therapy, the other is encouraged to become involved, since therapy is more likely to be successful if both spouses participate. There are no rigid requirements, and occasionally both spouses are evaluated separately during initial interviews before they agree to be seen together. A major requirement is that the couple has a goal—maintaining the marriage. At times, however, couples can be helped to achieve peaceful divorces.

The spouses are requested to complete a style-of-living analysis in the presence of each other. Such an analysis, based on childhood family constellation and atmosphere and on the interpretation of early recollections and childhood dreams, requires approximately three hours for each spouse. Upon its completion, an attempt is made to show how their lifestyles mesh and to discover the mutual attractions which fostered their initial cooperation but which no longer provide a basis for agreement. A therapeutic relationship is established rapidly by demonstrating very early in the first interview that something about each spouse and his unique form of uncooperativeness makes sense. The presence of two therapists who are also married seems to enhance this process. Often

125

one therapist, because of his past experience which he freely shares, can relate better to a given partner than the other therapist. Further, the therapists provide a model of a couple who have had and continue to have problems which were and can be solved. They may disagree sharply during the session and, therefore, demonstrate that disagreement does not need to be catastrophic and can be settled peacefully. They also provide an air of optimism, since both firmly believe that things can be changed. They tend to maintain a warm and friendly and, at times, almost humorous atmosphere during these sessions; though they follow a fairly specific pattern in early interviews, they are not adverse to improvising. Many couples seek help after one of them has been labeled by a previous therapist as "bad," "sick," "stupid," or "crazy." Since Adlerian techniques build on strengths and underplay weaknesses, while avoiding pseudoscientific diagnostic labels, the previously discouraged partner often leaves the first interview with a new lease on life and his partner frequently reconsiders him. Since the therapists do not function as judge and jury and the notion of guilt is de-emphasized, the personal burden for each partner is lessened.

Each spouse is asked to rate himself on a 1–5 scale in six life tasks: occupation, social relationships, love and marriage, getting along with oneself, finding one's place in the cosmos, and leisure and recreation. He is then asked how he thinks his partner would rate him, and, finally, his partner is asked to rate him. In this graphic way, the high blown ambitions or personal discouragement of each partner can be demonstrated. Each spouse is asked to imagine a ladder with ten rungs on which the top rung represents the ideal self and to place himself on the rung which represents his current self-esteem. Thus, low self-esteem, faulty goals, and personal discouragement become evident as the partners begin to look at one another in a new light.

As the first partner's lifestyle is summarized, all four members participate in the discussion, making suggestions and raising questions. To simplify the mechanics of the lifestyle analysis, one therapist usually asks most of the questions, while the other observes and records. These roles are, however, interchangeable. The therapist who has asked the questions dictates the summary of the childhood family atmosphere and constellation. The other therapist usually reads the previously recorded history, and all four members participate in the interpretation. A list of basic misconceptions is then drawn up and, when it is appropriate, the therapists relate these conclusions immediately to the present situation. The same procedure is repeated with the other partner, and, as his style-of-living unfolds, the areas of difficulty in the marriage are often dramatically pinpointed. In such an instance, the therapists may initiate a therapeutic reorientation if it seems appropriate.

The fifth or sixth interview is usually devoted to an evaluation of the lifestyles of the couple seeking therapy and reconsideration of the goals of therapy. Many alternatives are possible. In some cases, if the marital relationship has shown marked improvement, therapy may be terminated at this point; in other cases, therapy may continue, often on a less intensive basis. Whenever possible, the therapists should work intensively with the couple four to six hours a week during the first phase, but, later one hour a week of therapy is usually sufficient. Although the total duration of therapy may be twelve to fourteen hours, the couple should return for monthly "check-ups" during the following few months. Of course, the therapists are available to see the couple again if a new crisis appears.

Marital therapy with a therapist-couple is based on mutual respect— neither partner fighting nor giving in. The interactions between the therapist-couple should both demonstrate and validate the principle of mutual respect. A second task facing the therapists is to pinpoint the problem, since the couple's presenting problem is seldom the underlying or real one, which represents a threat to personal status or prestige and a concern over who is right. Sexual relations, money problems, childrearing, use of leisure time may have been chosen as the battlefield, but it is essential to avoid being sidetracked into long, nonproductive discussions about these apparent issues. The third task is to reach a new agreement based on helping each partner see what he can do. The wife may be adept at pointing out how the husband should change, while he knows exactly the ways in which she should be different. Each spouse is helped to see the part *he* is playing and to consider *his* alternatives. Humor is often helpful at this point, and the story of the lady psychiatrist in a crowded elevator may serve to lessen tension. The lady psychiatrist was suddenly aware that the man behind her in the elevator was poking at her. Her first reaction was to turn around and really tell him off, but she reconsidered, saying to herself, "Why should I? That's *his* problem!" Such stories have value through fixing the principle and through shared humor. In subsequent interviews a brief reference to the anecdote by any of the four participants may set off a round of laughter. Humor helps to create a relaxed, comfortable atmosphere and contributes to the shared enjoyment of the therapeutic process. The therapists, of course, must be sensitive to the feelings of the spouses in therapy and assure them that they are laughing with and not at them. The fourth task facing the therapists is to ensure that the shared decision of the couple will be carried out through mutual responsibility. Many couples feel that anything they decide upon must be for life, and it is helpful to encourage a short-term decision. In a week the decision may be reevaluated, for much can be learned from a bad decision. Reading a suitable book on marriage [2] can help a couple to pinpoint their problems and eventually to reach new agreements without the help of therapy.

Marital therapy with a therapist-couple is highly effective and economical in terms of time and money. An interesting aspect which is difficult to convey is that this particular form of therapy, in comparison to standard individual or group therapy, is almost a form of recreation. A joyous, cooperative atmosphere is achieved early in therapy and each forthcoming session is pleasantly anticipated. Although there may be some advantage in a male and female therapist-team who are not married to each other or in a therapist-team of the same sex, there is a certain camaraderie, a special mutual understanding, which exists when the therapist-team is also a marital team. Such a team is able to reveal itself as individuals *and* as a married couple during the course of therapy. Marital therapy by a therapist-couple may also be conducted with a group of couples in a manner similar to Adlerian family counseling.[1] Both parties need not be highly trained professionals as long as they have a cooperative working relationship and the lesser trained member does not feel inferior to the "professional" spouse.

REFERENCES

1. Deutsch, D.: Group therapy with married couples. *The Individ Psychol*, 4:56–62, 1967.
2. Dreikurs, R.: *The Challenge of Marriage*. New York, Duell, Sloan and Pearce, 1946.
3. Dreikurs, R., and Sonstegard, M. A.: The Adlerian or Teleoanalytic Group Counseling Approach. In Gazda, G. M. (Ed.): *Basic Approaches to Group Psychotherapy and Group Counseling*. Springfield, Thomas, 1968, pp. 197–232.

19

MULTIPLE THERAPY

Arthur G. Nikelly

THERAPY IS REFERRED TO as *multiple* when the client is treated simultaneously by more than one therapist. There is no single, rigid
procedure for conducting multiple psychotherapy. Fifty years ago Alfred
Adler treated children in the presence of a teacher, school counselor,
and social worker, and the children's school, or personal problems were
discussed openly and together. Children and young adults often respond
favorably to interpretations and suggestions regarding the causes of their
problems and the ways for changing them, especially if they are discussed in their presence but not addressed directly to them. When they
quickly realize that their problem is related not only to one or two other
persons, but that society as a whole is concerned and indirectly affected
by their difficulty, they become cognizant of the appropriate seriousness
of their problem. Likewise, clients gain insights into their behavior from
listening to therapists formulate the dynamic factors associated with
their problem, in a manner similar to members in group psychotherapy.
Adler's method has been adopted by many of his followers, particularly
Dreikurs [2] and his associates, who have since developed and applied the
techniques of multiple therapy more systematically and with considerable therapeutic effectiveness.

Whether in a school, clinic, or hospital situation, the client should
first be interviewed by a therapist who obtains information on his
current problems, on the precipitating circumstances and factors immediately relevant to the situation. He is then advised of the benefit of
another consultant's opinion and referred to a second therapist or

interviewer for further evaluation. The second therapist or interviewer attempts to explore the background and developmental factors in the life of the client, such as family constellation, sibling order, social interactions, and other significant experiences and events since childhood. In the third session he is seen by both therapists, who summarize their clinical impressions in the client's presence, and invite him to comment, and elaborate upon them. More avenues for exploration open, since the client may challenge or disagree with his therapists. The sessions may alternate from single to multiple therapists and the client can eventually be transferred easily into group therapy. Thus inertia is prevented and the client is encouraged to become an active participant in therapy. Another way of resolving an impasse through the use of multiple therapy is to ask for the client's permission to invite another consultant to temporarily participate in order "to see if he can help us out for a while until we can get started again." The client's anxieties about having another therapist present, particularly that this may make his problem seem more "serious," should be alleviated by explaining to him beforehand the purpose of multiple psychotherapy.

Therapists may play different roles depending upon the client's main problems. For instance, one therapist can play the father role, while the other may assume the role of the brother or "pal," and the same principle applies with a therapist of the opposite sex. Roles can be shifted so that the client may become less sensitive to figures with whom he has difficulty. Since the presence of two or three therapists affords greater opportunity for him to reveal more aspects of himself, easier recognition of his lifestyle and the dynamic formulation of his problem is apt to be reached more rapidly and accurately. In addition, depending on the client and the nature of his problem, one therapist may play a passive and the other an active role, or one may present the problem as the client sees it, and the other may analyze and interpret the problem from a professional viewpoint. The presence of more than three therapists, however, may sometimes be less effective, since some clients, particularly children, may feel threatened in being cross-examined, and may become more guarded and defensive. Since the participating therapists are subjected to a more personally involved and intimate experience, they become both more accepting of each other and more mature in their clinical skills. Multiple psychotherapy assists in the awareness of their own motivations and defenses, as if they were participating in some kind of a modified form of group didactic analysis, through which they come to understand each other as much as the client. Tensions and disagreements which may arise among therapists during sessions with the client, should be explored more thoroughly after the session is over. Even if mistakes in technique are recognized, they should not be bluntly pointed out in a critical manner before the client. Disagreements and differing viewpoints have an appropriate place in multiple therapy insofar as they occur for the benefit of the client and not for proving some theoretical position.

Dreikurs [1] maintains that there are several advantages to multiple rather than individual psychotherapy, especially with recalcitrant, anxious clients, or when therapy comes to a standstill. The client feels that he is receiving greater service and relating with more professional authority, and the greater concern shown makes him feel appreciated and important. He is encouraged to display cooperation, to become more involved and to share in the therapy process without danger of developing dependency on one therapist. Setbacks are prevented, since he is invited to interact with two different personalities and to see how he can improve regarding the expectations of others. He develops greater flexibility in his thoughts and actions, and he understands how he affects and impresses people. Therapists can check their interpretations, and can readily recognize what the other is missing or not doing. Multiple psychotherapy enhances objectivity as new viewpoints are elicited and exchanged, and the client can acquire insights as he observes his therapists disagree and participates in their dialogue whenever he wishes. He has an opportunity to reevaluate and to develop more realistic expectations of himself as he is given verbal feedback from his therapists. Finally, he sees how his therapists interact with each other in an atmosphere of mutual equality, and, by realizing that they too are human beings, he appraises himself in a more favorable way.

Haigh and Kell [3] suggest the usefulness of holding pretherapy and posttherapy briefing sessions, especially if the case is particularly difficult or critical. The relationship between therapists must be harmonious, since they are expected to respect, compliment, and assist each other just as they do with the client. Ultimately, they should serve as models for the client to emulate. Consequently, therapists having personal or professional conflicts with each other are not encouraged to engage in multiple therapy. By eliminating competitiveness and fostering cooperation, there is greater rapport among the therapists and the client, for they feel sure of themselves since the constant threat of being judged is eliminated. Haigh and Kell also point out that the treatment of one client by two or three therapists affords the active participation of less experienced therapists and provides an ideal training arrangement. Warkentin *et al.*[4] maintain that multiple psychotherapy helps the client feel safer and less guilty of expressed hostility or anger, because it is being directed collectively to several therapists. In addition, it instills more confidence to be able to talk to several persons at once, especially if the problem involves relating to people. Favoritism shown by the client, or his attempted manipulation of the therapists, can be quite revealing concerning his lifestyle, but he should be encouraged to work out his problems with whichever therapist this favoritism is directed. Tact is required so that the therapist and the client do not feel constantly "under the gun." Finally, the therapists must never monopolize the session or try to test their pet theories, but should always give the client "equal time." He must feel part of a cooperative team rather than as a person being "treated" by an outside group of "experts."

Other benefits of multiple psychotherapy are that it forces the client to share in the responsibility for self-understanding and maturity, and to participate more openly in therapy. It prevents him from escaping the real issues by sidetracking into intellectual discussions or irrelevant areas. In addition, it also prevents the development of transference and particularly countertransference, identification with the client is reduced, and the relationship between therapists and client is less apt to become superficial. Although thresholds of psychological sensitivity vary among therapists, such differences are minimized in a multiple therapy situation, and personal frustration often encountered in a single therapist is thwarted. The school situation is ideal for multiple counseling, since teachers and counselors can interview and discuss the student's problem conjointly with him. Trainees in counseling or psychiatry can benefit by actively participating in a session with their supervisor and the client. In hospital and other clinical settings, nurses, physicians, and mental health personnel often engage in multiple therapy when they participate in staff conferences and discuss the client's problem right in his presence. Psychiatrists administering medication to a client who is being treated regularly by a psychologist or social worker may want to hold joint sessions to review progress in therapy. In such cases the client often responds to encouragement and exhibits motivation for change.

REFERENCES

1. Dreikurs, R.: Techniques and dynamics of multiple psychotherapy. *Psychiat Quart, 24:*788–799, 1950.
2. Dreikurs, R., *et al.*: "Patient-therapist relationship in multiple therapy, I and II." *Psychiat Quart, 26:*219–227; 590–596, 1952.
3. Haigh, Gerard, and Kell, Bill L.: Multiple therapy as a method for training and research in psychotherapy. *J. Abnorm Psychol, 45:*659–666, 1950.
4. Warkentin, John, *et al.*: A comparison of individual and multiple psychotherapy. *Psychiatry, 14:*415–418, 1951.

20

PSYCHODRAMA

Arthur G. Nikelly and Adaline Starr

PSYCHODRAMA is the reenactment of a life situation in which the individual's relationships, real or imagined, are acted out in the form of a role which he chooses to portray. Other "actors" with whom he interacts in a particular conflict may portray or symbolize persons in life with whom he is experiencing difficulties. A client enacts important areas of his life with members of the audience playing the roles of the absent persons. These audience participants may also serve as a "sounding board" on whom he expresses his difficulties and who, in turn, collectively provide him with a corrective and reality-oriented reaction containing a plausible solution to his problem. Other clients in the audience can identify and share in the protagonist's feelings and emotions. Psychodrama aims toward the accurate portrayal of the client's present, past, and future actions. The client's self-expression and freedom of communication leads to self-understanding and personality reorientation. Although psychodrama is not considered an Adlerian technique, it may be used, often without the client's full awareness, to evoke his movement and to bring out his lifestyle. Psychodrama has diagnostic value and offers the client solutions to his problems in a manner analogous to group psychotherapy, in which the client also receives feedback from the other members of the group.

The client's life roles are formed through his private and collective world, and his personality identity develops from them. Growth de-

The editor wishes to acknowledge constructive comments on an earlier version of this chapter by Nahum E. Shoobs.

135

pends upon knowing and fulfilling the expectations of age roles. Role playing is a unit of behavior and may be used as a diagnostic tool and/or a training method. While actors are capable of acting a role imposed upon them, a client with personal problems actually enacts his *real* self with an involved, spontaneous, and intense feeling. Role playing helps him to express intensely and exactly how he feels, how he sees himself and others, and the feelings which he thinks others have toward him. By portraying others as he sees them and by putting himself in their places, he becomes less sensitive toward others and their influence over him may lessen. The purpose of psychodrama is to achieve a satisfactory solution to the interpersonal dilemma—the solving of a real-life problem through self-exploration.

A psychodrama session begins as the group decides what problem to use and who will be the participating members. A structured plot can be used which contains the client's particular conflict. As a protagonist emerges, he can enact his problem before the group and select individual persons or auxiliary egos who symbolize specific persons in his life. He can also be asked to enact the responses of these significant individuals by anticipating what he thinks they will do. Later, he will be exposed to their actual responses to his problem, and his awareness of these differences in response will make him more aware of himself. On the other hand, if the protagonist merely acts one given role, only catharsis and release from tension may result. The client's underlying difficulties may become more apparent to the therapist who can then assign him to play encounters in which he becomes more fully aware of his actions. Psychodrama then becomes a training and a teaching technique. As the client describes a situation, the therapist may interrupt: "Don't tell us; show us what happened." Another initial procedure is to ask, "How did you come to know of this session? Why don't you come up here and tell the group?"

The members can be seated in a living room arrangement, in a semicircle, or on a stage. The therapist may suggest simple and structured situations through which the clients can practice in order to increase their familiarity with this technique and to stimulate group interaction. The therapist should encourage spontaneous expression and invite comment on the qualities which each member attempts to enact. Persons with similar difficulties ordinarily are not grouped together, since passive clients, for instance, may experience enormous difficulty in enacting roles while aggressive adolescents may become destructive or dominate the group.

The members are encouraged to become familiar with each other at their own rate of speed and to discuss areas of personal interest and mutual concern before starting. The therapist can suggest more diverse roles to be portrayed in the plot. He need not be familiar with each client's dynamics and lifestyle but is prepared to evaluate it as it emerges. Later, he may want to place together opposite personalities (an aggressive child reacting to a passive parent surrogate) in order that the resulting clash will elicit solutions and insights from the audience or the auxiliary egos. The client may wish to portray a character from his life which has affected him or continues to do so, or to enact a role that takes place in a situation with which he wishes to cope. It is often beneficial for each member to play a solo role or a soliloquy as a preliminary experience.

The psychotherapist can ask individual members to switch roles after he has seen their lifestyles in action, so that their respective goals can be more clearly seen. As a new situation is created, alternate responses become necessary; should these be inadequate, the client's partners, who see him from the outside, can point this out to him. It is permissible for the therapist to assume an active role in a particular plot to make members feel more comfortable, but, in such an instance, another person should assume the director's role. The audience may serve as a chorus and be comprised of "veteran actors" who are trained to "echo" the underlying purpose or motive of the client as he acts out his part. Through this device, his perception of the situation changes and he is encouraged to find new ways to cope.

Roles vary depending upon the client's age, sex, social situation, personality make-up, and the nature of his peer, sibling, or marital relationships. The therapist himself may enact the behavior of a person with whom the client is having difficulties; as the client sees how his actions appear to others, he gains new insights and can respond differently to similar figures in other settings. The therapist can act as a father, a teacher, or other authority figure to an adolescent client, for instance, so that he can work out a new relationship based on a better understanding of his interactions with such figures. When the client's lifestyle is evident to the therapist, he can assign another member of the group to act as a "chorus" to echo and reinforce the client's intentions and private logic. In this way, the error of the client's private logic can be dispelled. While the therapist can play a specific role for a client, it is better to have an auxiliary ego do it so that the director is free to act as catalyst, chief therapist, and to summarize the events of the session.

"Auxiliary egos" serve to support and guide the client and to remind him of the roles required of him by society. Through them he is encouraged to invalidate private logic, belief, and purposes which do not have consensual validation. In a similar way, another member of the group may mirror the client so that he can see himself in action. Rehearsing anticipated or anxiety-invoking situations (a date or a confrontation with an employer) reveals the client's self-concept, goals, and safeguard mechanisms which can then be modified by the auxiliary egos and the therapist.[1]

In essence, psychodrama enables the client to act out his problems, and, consequently, to deal more effectively with interpersonal situations. Through role playing he reveals his lifestyle and, after constructive reorientation, is able to originate alternate solutions to a present situation. While the principles of psychodrama apply to people of all ages, the therapist uses a different emphasis with various age groups. With children the therapist is more active and can assign roles since children are more apt to act out their impulses in fantasy than in reality. The therapist may find a greater spontaneity in adolescents and adults who see a real reason for participating in psychodrama. Starr[2] describes an excellent procedure for applying psychodramatic techniques with children.

Married couples often provide excellent psychodramatic groups, not only for purposes of catharsis, but also as a means of eliciting the lifestyles of the respective spouses which the therapist can then reflect to each partner, asking him in turn to reflect it back to his mate. This technique can provide couples with new insights in coping with each other's style of life—a crucial factor in marital counseling since divergent lifestyles are often the greatest source of difficulty in marriage. When one spouse contends that he understands the other's lifestyle, he is asked to reenact it; this mirror or reversal technique will show whether or not he really understands his spouse. Role-playing techniques, incidentally, can also be used for educational purposes in history, sociology, and psychology classes where students can enact historical figures, members of minority groups, or emotionally disturbed persons.

REFERENCES

1. Moreno, J. L., and Kipper, David A.: Group Psychodrama and Community Centered Counseling. In Gazda, George M. (Ed.): *Basic Approaches to Group Psychotherapy and Group Counseling.* Springfield, Ill., Thomas, 1968, pp. 27–79.
2. Starr, A.: Psychodrama in the Child Guidance Centers. In Dreikurs, R.; Corsini, R.; Lowe, R., and Sonstegard, M. (Eds.): *Adlerian Family Counseling.* Eugene, Oreg., University of Oregon Press, 1959, pp. 75–81.

Part V   Special
Syndrome
Techniques

21

THE PAMPERED LIFESTYLE

Leo Rattner

Alfred Adler emphasized two basic variations of neurotic personality development—the lifestyles of the rejected child and the pampered child. The thesis of the rejected child—and the influence of rejection on the etiology of neuroses—was easily understood and accepted, but the significance of pampering was often overlooked. In his final writings, he often asserted that pampering was spreading rapidly through Western civilization and becoming the most prevalent neurotic interaction between parent and child. A psychological definition of pampering is doing for the child what he is physically or mentally able to do for himself.

Pampering, then, depends on the situational context. It is perfectly normal to help a three-year-old child tie his shoelaces, but this action becomes pampering when the child is six years old. It might be reasonable to give a child some assistance with his homework during the first school years; it is pampering when a parent does homework for a fifth-grader or sixth-grader. Assisting the child is justified; taking over for the child becomes pampering. The denial of the child's spontaneous desire for activity, the systematic discouragement that results from substituting parental action for the child's own endeavor, produces the peculiar configuration which we call the pampered lifestyle.

The pampered lifestyle develops an attitude of expectation and demand for pampering.[2] The individual insists on special privileges for himself. The pampered lifestyle is characterized by the desire to grasp, to accumulate, to take from others, but not to give of oneself. The

143

pampered child, like the rejected child, denies that social usefulness can be a valid basis for social interaction.[3]

Pampering is, of course, deeply embedded in our contemporary materialistic civilization and is constantly reinforced by prevailing values. Advertising slogans which speak of the "good life" refer primarily to the accumulation of material possessions and often cater to the seemingly universal desire to get something for nothing. The good life that is propagated by radio and television commercials seem to have no connection with truth, beauty, and justice, or with a striving for excellence. Rather, we are invited to remain fixated forever on the level of childhood. "Pamper yourself," says a widely-used advertising slogan.

There are many factors that account for the prevalence of pampering as a dominant educational technique in our time. The most important reason is that children have no clear-cut role to play in our society. Parents are confused about what to demand and expect of children and may treat them as precocious, premature adults or as funny creatures who will remain forever on an infantile level. Rarely does there seem to be respect for the child as a growing, maturing person who should be given increasing responsibilities as he develops his physical and mental capacities.

In part, this misconception in the treatment of children is an inevitable outcome of urban, industrialized civilization. Children no longer constitute an intrinsic material asset as they did in a rural society and must now be accepted for their own sake, not as a material asset but because they are wanted. In fact, they are often pampered because they are intrinsically without value to the parents, a situation thinly disguised by the pampering relationship. In the absence of a mature, loving relationship, children may become objects on which parents act out their neurotic frustrations and conflicts.[4] Children are capable of perceiving this exploitation and react with constantly increasing demands for pampering in a desperate attempt to force parents to recognize that the child is not completely worthless. Through his behavior, the pampered child says, "If we can't love each other, at least let us play this neurotic game together." Unhappily for parents and children, the parasitic relationship of pampering is increasingly becoming the only area where children can develop and retain a semblance of autonomy and self-respect. Strength and power resides in the fact that the child can make demands on the parents and force them to accede to these demands.

The tragedy of all pampered people is that they restrict themselves to the minimum use of their resources and capacities rather than trying to attain the maximum. The essence of the pampered lifestyle is an exploiting, enslaving attitude toward the environment. The pampered person seems to ask one overriding question of the people around him: "What can you do for me?" Psychologically speaking, he uses his symptoms to blackmail his environment.

While most of us are tainted by the pampered lifestyle, for many people it constitutes the core of existence. With brilliant insight, Alfred Adler recognized that criminals often possess a pampered lifestyle.[1] They express their demand for pampering with an argument that is frequently used to justify their criminal activities: "I have been victimized in my childhood, and, therefore, I am allowed to take what I want." Similarly, addicts, alcoholics, people who habitually overeat suffer from the same syndrome. The world has refused to honor their claim for pampering, but they have found a solution that is quite satisfactory for them. Individuals possessed of a pampered lifestyle suffer from a host of syndromes and, clinically speaking, the old labels of neuroses, psychoses, and personality disorders are rather meaningless when applied to these people. *The pampered lifestyle is the central feature of their maladjustment.* From the Adlerian point of view, nothing can be accomplished until this lifestyle changes.

The pampered person is emotionally discouraged and spiritually crippled. He has a hesitant approach toward the problems of life and avoids realistic solutions for them. Anxieties and phobias are prevalent clinical symptoms but are not the result of traumatic experiences, as psychoanalytic interpretations would have it. Rather, these symptoms must be seen as integral to the pampered lifestyle. Anxieties and phobias are exploited to justify the avoidance of life's problems and serve as convenient rationalizations: "Since I am afraid of crowds, of open spaces, of height, of physical illness—how can I be expected to get married or to be successful in my work?" Yet, precisely because a realistic solution of life's problems cannot be attempted as long as these symptoms persist, they are held onto and defended with utmost tenacity.

The pampered client is not interested in getting well. He blames the world—his parents, his family, and other social institutions—for his own shortcomings. Why should he adjust to this hateful society that, from his point of view, is responsible for most of his troubles? Why should he allow himself to be deprived of such convenient rationalizations for his own failure to become a well-adjusted person?

It is an important part of therapy to expose and to clarify these rationalizations. While it may be true that parents helped to create the pathogenic situation, they cannot continue to be blamed. The pampered client clings to his neurotic lifestyle because of strong feelings of hostility towards his parents. With his failures, he punishes them over and over again. With his neurotic behavior he says: "Since you did not let me grow up to become a mature person, I shall forever remain a dependent but hostile child." A vicious spitefulness permeates all his actions.

The therapist must be aware of two major problems in the treatment of pampered people. One is the profound discouragement of the pampered client which is generally far more pronounced than in similar cases of neurotic disturbances. The pampered person does not believe himself capable of *any* constructive achievement. Thus, in the beginning of therapy, considerable time must be spent on support and encouragement. Discouraging situations must be avoided, since any defeat will have an adverse effect on his self-esteem. On the other hand, the pampered client must be constantly encouraged to tackle any problem for which he is realistically prepared by way of training and emotional readiness to find a solution. Only when he experiences competence in a tangible way can he learn to overcome his feelings of inferiority.

The second problem stems from the exploiting attitude employed by the pampered client in all human relationships. He wants to take without giving anything in return, and he brings this attitude to the therapeutic relationship. In subtle ways, he demands that the therapist maintain the pampering relationship that the client had with his parents. He will invariably ask for special privileges. He will try to get preferential treatment in the payment of fees. He will try to prolong the duration of his session at the expense of his competitors—the other patients. Finally, he will try to get the therapist to tell him what he ought to do. With a variety of tricky questions and behavior mechanisms, he will try to push the therapist into a parental position so that the pampered person can claim credit for his successes but can blame the therapist for his failures.

The treatment of the person with a pampered lifestyle is not essentially different from the treatment of other neurotics or cases of personality disorders. The therapist must gain the client's confidence. Together they must explore and understand his personality and attitudes, the ways in which he relates to himself and the world. They must learn to comprehend his lifestyle and the problems and difficulties caused by it. The pampered lifestyle and the need for self-pampering must be emphasized in the therapist's interpretations, for only when this basic condition is thoroughly understood can the client make a realistic effort to change his personality. Awareness and insight precede change. Without the realization of the destructive consequences of his pampered lifestyle, no client will ever willingly give up his neurotic symptoms.

Psychotherapy is an art as well as a science, and no formula can capture the essence of this process. The therapist must experience each client as an individual and respond to him spontaneously without preconceived notions. If the therapist deceives himself by believing that he has found the one correct way of dealing with pampering, he is likely to be taught an uncomfortable lesson. His clients will teach him that this vision of godlikeness does not correspond with reality and that human beings are not inclined to live up to stereotyped concepts of how they ought to behave.

Free associations, dream interpretations, and other traditional devices may be used in therapy, but are employed to further the analysis of the pampered lifestyle and not as ends in themselves. Interpretations that do not lead to a change in lifestyle are meaningless. It is not enough to give an elegant interpretation of a dream or of a particular past event. Rather, the past must be understood in order to relate it dynamically to the present and future, and the client must understand that when the past is comprehended and meaningfully related to present problems he has an obligation to change. Perhaps one of the reasons why orthodox psychoanalysis takes such a long time is that this elementary supposition is not clearly established and does not become the fundamental basis of therapeutic interaction.

Psychotherapy is an organic process, and changes are gradual and slow. The habits of a lifetime are not changed easily, but when problems are sufficiently explored and understood, when the neurotic rationalizations of the pampered lifestyle have been exposed and refuted, we often witness an amazing change. Where escape had been the rule, forward movement is now in evidence. Where fear had governed actions, new courage and resolution are apparent. In short, where neurotic symptoms had obscured self-perception and perception of others, a healthy, functioning personality now emerges.

To bring about these changes, the therapist must grasp the intricacies of the pampered lifestyle. Like a skillful tactician he determines at which point the pampered lifestyle can best be attacked and dislodged. In this situation, the therapist can be likened to the Greek scientist Archimedes who looked for a fulcrum from which he could uproot the universe. The therapist, more modestly, tries only to uproot the pampered individual's universe by exposing its neurotic foundations and the inevitable suffering it creates. When the client is ready to change, the therapist must guide such willingness to the task of attacking the pampered lifestyle. The criterion of successful psychotherapy is the client's readiness to give up his demands for pampering. As long as the demand for pampering or self-pampering persists, the client cannot be considered a truly mature person.[5]

There are two major obstacles to the successful resolution of the pampered lifestyle. One is the cynical attitude of the pampered person. He distrusts everybody and sees human relationships only in terms of exploitation. In his view, the stronger person always rules and exploits the weaker one, and he is invariably suspicious of the motives of others. He does not believe that anyone could be truly interested in helping him, since he himself has no interest in the welfare of others. He will repeatedly test the therapist, trying to expose him as a selfish and greedy individual. In subtle ways he will try to confirm his basic view of human relations—that the psychologist, like everybody else, is concerned only with personal prestige and the accumulation of money. It would suit the client well to confirm this view, for if the therapist can be proved selfish, the client is not required to change. "Why should I alone become more social-minded," his argument runs, "when everybody else is only out for himself?" His argument carries considerable strength and conviction, since many examples in our society corroborate this view; and it is imperative that the therapist have worked through his personal problems and acquired a mature social interest so that he is able to cope realistically and successfully with the client's challenge.

The second obstacle comes from the fusion of the pampered lifestyle with the drive for personal power. All pampered persons cherish power and are unwilling to give up whatever power they possess in controlling their environment. Without the power to exact pampering, they would feel completely inadequate. A sudden withdrawal of pampering may lead to a breakdown and mental illness. In therapy, this danger is avoided by gradually building up the client's courage and self-confidence. Setting realistic goals is an important part of this process. As he achieves constructive results, his need for neurotic power diminishes. He begins to realize that he does not need special privileges in order to make an effort to contribute his share to the welfare of the community.

Therapy becomes feasible when the pampered person faces a critical problem for which his lifestyle offers no solution. In a crisis situation the inadequacies of the pampered lifestyle become clearly visible. No longer can rationalizations be employed to hide the lack of preparedness for communal living. In an existentialist sense, the pampered person has to recognize the absurdity of his existence; yet, these feelings of despair and hopelessness also offers the best prognosis for the eventual success of therapy. Psychotherapy becomes effective when the client is aware of his suffering and understands the connection between his suffering and his pampered lifestyle. Awareness alone, however, is not sufficient, and a choice must be made between mental health and the continuation of pampering. A choice affirmative of life is more likely to be made when the client's lifestyle has been clarified in the therapeutic process and his motivations for continuing it have been brought into consciousness. Even the most hardened neurotic has a difficult time maintaining destructive attitudes when he begins to realize that he is exploiting his environment and hurting himself in the process.

Psychotherapy is an efficient and rational instrument for dealing with the pampered lifestyle. Adlerian therapy can be especially effective in treating the syndrome of pampering, provided the therapist recognizes and avoids the pitfalls of a pampering relationship with the client. But therapy reaches relatively few people and cannot cope with the underlying social problems. It cannot ameliorate the social conditions that foster and reinforce the pampered lifestyle.

REFERENCES

1. Adler, A.: *The Science of Living.* Edited by H. L. Ansbacher. New York, Doubleday, 1969, pp. 6–9.
2. Adler, A.: *Superiority and Social Interest.* Edited by H. L. and Rowena R. Ansbacher, Evanston, Ill., Northwestern University Press, 1964, pp. 195–197.
3. Adler, A.: *Social Interest: A Challenge to Mankind.* New York, Capricorn Books, 1964, pp. 144–155.
4. Dreikurs, R.: *The Challenge of Parenthood.* New York, Duell, Sloan and Pearce, 1948, pp. 97–102.
5. Way, L.: *Adler's Place in Psychology.* New York, Macmillan, 1950, pp. 209–211.

22

THE SELF-BOUND LIFESTYLE

Esther P. Spitzer

I N OUR AGE of dropouts from society, there emerges the passive, with-drawn, self-bound individual who avoids commitment and fears close emotional ties. Our competitive society, geared to success, imposes a special handicap on this type who must constantly compare himself with assertive and aggressive persons. Instead of looking vertically at others as above or below him, a destructive habit that poisons his personal relationships, he can be encouraged to look horizontally at others as equals who may be different in their needs and abilities. If he is to make comparisons, it is far better that he measure his present with his past achievements.

The techniques described here have in the writer's experience spurred self-bound clients to mobilize their inner creativity and are based on such concepts as goals, early memories, social interest, dreams and the use of humor. It goes without saying that no technique works without therapist-client rapport, for the withdrawn client, out of fear of ridicule and rejection, has barricaded himself behind a wall and has substituted obsessive order, perfectionism, and fantasy for participation in life.[2]

Timing is of crucial importance, and what works with one client may be inappropriate or destructive with another. The client is first required to formulate his goals. What does he want from therapy and from life? He may write these goals out in his own words and refer to them, especially when he gets off the track. The psychiatrist, Norman L. Paul, considers the first objective in therapy to be the termination of therapy. This point of view is in line with the general systems theory; set your

151

objective first and then work backwards. What is required to achieve your objective?

Clients who have never asked themselves where they are going and what they want out of life often come up with rather vague answers—happiness, marriage, success. Some, out of confusion and apathy, admit they do not know what they want and that is why they came for therapy. Others glibly state one goal but act on another hidden goal. A gifted painter, for instance, chafing in a well-paying job, unrelated to his artistic talent, states that his goal is "to be happy, to get along with people, and to be free of tension." Inadvertently, he hints he likes to own a Rolls Royce because his uncle owns one.

Adler maintained that no one can change his lifestyle without changing his picture of the world.[1] The painter, in the example cited above, operated on the mistaken premise that money alone brings happiness. He was shown that happiness comes from finding satisfaction in one's family, friends, and work. Once he understood that he was trying to move in two directions—one toward self-realization as a painter and the other toward acquiring wealth—he returned to his original vocation of painting and lost his psychosomatic symptoms. Such clients can be asked to consider what happens when one signals a horse to go right and left at the same time. They quickly get the point.

Men and women often give marriage as their goal but show by too casual sex relations, by bouts of promiscuity, and by their dreams a preference for romance and a fear of the exclusive commitment and total involvement demanded by marriage. Their distrust of the opposite sex and an inordinate fear of rejection have to be resolved before they feel free to select a suitable mate—a person who is available for marriage and shows a capacity to sustain a relationship.

One brilliant, cultured girl had such a distrust of all men who symbolized her passive, ineffectual father. After every abortive affair she would deluge the therapist with what she called "lesbian dreams about women." She was assured that she was not lesbian, that her dreams symbolically reflected her abject despair at coping with men. For the first time she was able to answer the ubiquitous question—"Why do I always pick the wrong man?" Her fear of emotional closeness impelled her to choose detached, undemanding people. She was shown that, in order to come close to herself, she must first come close to her own feelings of love, grief, fear, and anger. She also had to learn how to communicate with men in ways other than bodily contact, how to initiate conversation instead of relying solely on her looks to interest men. She was encouraged to practice initiating comment on newspapers, books, and the theatre with the therapist instead of waiting for cues from others. In time she mustered enough courage to communicate in this manner with others. The ensuing rise in her self-esteem made her more discriminating with men; she learned to delay sexual gratification until common interests and values had been established. The necessity for learning the rudiments of interpersonal relationships so mortified her pride that she needed to be consoled. The therapist assured her that she was simply a late bloomer and that, like the chrysanthemum, late blossoms have a special beauty. Cheerfully, she declared that although she might be late, at least she would "bloom."

A client, working in the evenings toward an advanced degree, was totally unaware of the effect of his aloofness on his co-workers until, through psychodrama, he was asked to act out the part of a co-worker. Stymied at first to the point of speechlessness, he began to laugh at himself as he imagined a fellow worker growling, "What's eating the big stiff? Wait until he gets his Ph.D. He won't even look at us, much less talk to us." The therapist pantomimed his fear of closeness by thrusting out her elbows with the warning, "Danger! Don't come close. Keep away!" Paradoxically, he was so preoccupied with his own fears of rejection that the thought that others might construe his aloofness as rejection had never occurred to him.

Withdrawn, elderly persons with self-bound lifestyles respond remarkably when their faulty goals are corrected and they are encouraged to develop socially useful ones that bring them back to the community. The recovery of status and function brings zest back to them. Thus, a person discovers that only by losing himself in pursuit of a healthy goal can he find himself. By supplying a missing goal or replacing a faulty one, the therapist can often reverse depression, break isolation, and restore health and self-confidence.[3]

Early memories, often by their very selectivity, can foreshadow the client's schizoid lifestyle. A girl of twenty-one recalls that at age three she stood behind her mother rocking in a chair and watched the rhythm with trance-like fascination. Suddenly, the leg of the rocker crushed the girl's foot. At her outcry, the mother, instead of comforting the girl, added abuse and anger to injury. The girl remained a spectator, an onlooker behind someone's back, instead of a participant. Her fascination with rhythms showed a rich fantasy life, which had to be explored and exposed as a substitute for struggle with reality. She had become adept at observing and analyzing people, in order to eliminate and reject them, and had to be encouraged to look at the nice things about other people instead of carping at their flaws and foibles.

Picture the low degree of social interest of the client who ignores the seat opposite the therapist to curl up on a sofa in the farthest corner of the room. After an invitation to take the chair opposite the therapist, she is encouraged to explore her need for distance from people. Sometimes the client informs you with a vaunting pride in her uniqueness that she is not a "joiner." Indeed, the word "join" may be such an anathema to the withdrawn client that she may be lost to the therapist who mentions the word prematurely. Involvement in her own problems was made through open-ended questions ("What is a good relationship?" "What is the meaning of acceptance?") whose answers were found within herself, not in a book. Nature abhors a vacuum, so, in order to grow, a person, a part of nature, needs some meaningful human contact and feedback. Even if the responses were merely on an intellectual level, the therapist's concern with the client's growth stimulates self-involvement in her problem and kindles a hope that conditions do not have to remain as they are.

The client may be further roused from apathy and emotional numbness by the questions, "How do you see yourself now?" and "How do you see yourself in five or ten years?" The latter question is a remarkable divining rod to plumb and disclose hidden goals, a faulty lifestyle, or the expectation of magical solution to problems. Above all, the questions must never be presented with overtones of criticism or judgment, since the client is already overburdened with self-disparagement. The therapist needs to assure her that, although he does not have all the answers to problems, he is a collaborator who is always on the client's side.

Explaining dreams can help a self-bound client understand himself. The withdrawn person is apt to be too suspicious to be an effusive talker, but by garnering bits of family history, fragments of lifestyle, goals, information on his position among siblings or on the people he likes most, and possibly an account of a dream, the therapist can initiate a response in the schizoid client. Dreams can indicate how the client feels about himself and therapy. As a kind of closure, the therapist can commend the client for his courage and creativity in the face of childhood reverses and for his present decision to build his own destiny rather than to drift or wallow in despair.

The client who displays reticence and a stiff posture may be asked at the end of the first session how he feels. "I haven't learned a damn thing!" said one, to which the therapist replied, "I accept your feelings and I like and respect your candor." This client obviously regarded therapy as an intellectual experience instead of the beginning of a close relationship with an authentic human being who is consistent and stable and who accepts him as he is at the moment. Only through close relatedness can a self-bound person learn to know what love is. This same client reported at his next session, "Something happened to me in the subway right after I left you. All the pain and stiffness in my neck I've had for a year suddenly disappeared. My wife says it's the first time in years that she saw me take a nap."

Dreams are a singularly felicitous way of involving the withdrawn person in his own problems, since he sees the dream as something of his own creation in the language of imagery. His dream often shows his inadequate way of solving his problem and, like a dress rehearsal, illustrates how he anticipates the future. Clients who deplore their lack of dreams can be encouraged to relate their fantasies, since both manifestations metaphorically answer the question, "What would happen if . . . ?"

Adeptness in fathoming one's own dreams can be cultivated. A passive, shy client dreams his girl is entering a convent. "Am I sending her to a nunnery before she can jilt me?" he asks. Another client with recurring dreams of rescuing people from a concentration camp, a fire, or drowning interprets, "How unworthy I must feel inside to want to dazzle my girl with such feats of bravery!" Actually, he is not brave but a coward who recoils from the risk of rejection, who communicates both verbally and nonverbally his low self-regard, who always undersells himself in a way that invites rejection. A change in his self-image enabled him to date a more suitable girl.

Schizoid clients who restrain their feelings and cannot express anger can be encouraged to vent some of their grievance onto an empty chair where, in imagination, sits a person with whom they cannot relate openly and candidly. The therapist can explain that parents, for example, can be forgiven only after rage against them is experienced and accepted as one's own. A therapist, however, should wait for cues from dreams or fantasy before resorting to this drastic form of catharsis.

Humor can often serve as a sword to cut through the Gordian knot of the client's conflict. He can be shown how humor builds perspective and enlarges his repetoire of behavior. His current ineffective behavior can be challenged: "Let's see how differently you could have reacted to this situation." Humor can also be used as an antidote to self-pity and the tendency to ruminate on injustice.

As for the ubiquitous "injustice collector" who surfeits the therapist with accounts of people who abuse him, the therapist can at a certain point ask, "Am I too on your list?" At another point he can inquire, "When will you get wise and throw away your list?" The client full of obsessive doubts and indecisions when embarking on a new venture may be asked, "Are you looking for a map? There is none. You're in new, unexplored territory." The client may counter, "But how do I know I'll succeed?" "If you must enjoy these orgies of self-doubts," the therapist may reply, "give yourself half an hour of this torment, then put it behind you as finished business."

Weeping during a therapy session can signify a pampered lifestyle or a healthy emergence of feeling. The client often uses "water power" to accuse the therapist, as if to say, "Why don't you take away my neurosis?" The therapist should explain to him that his neurosis was his early choice in coping with life's difficulties and that new emotional habits must be built, such as taking risks, using humor, being honest, and accepting one's feelings. He can be told that growth develops in stages, and often these stages may not be bypassed with impunity. The client may give self-pity as his reason for crying, but rarely does he mention that the tears may also indicate his anger with the therapist's slowness, an anger which is a projection of his own impatient desire for quick, easy solutions. If the client does express anger toward the therapist, the therapist must remind him that no one can change another human being, not even God Himself, unless a person wants to change.

The positive value of tears was demonstrated by a withdrawn, intellectual, dependent client who held such a rigid taboo on the expression of feeling that he did not permit himself to experience anger when insulted by his wife at a party. After a year of therapy he broke down in tears and felt ashamed and apologized. It was the first time he had come close to his feeling for himself as a person, for his loneliness and isolation. His too frequent calls for advice between sessions impelled the therapist to require that he sleep on a problem before phoning. To stimulate trust in his own judgment he was told that if, after waiting fifteen minutes, he thought about his problem, he could answer his own questions.

The withdrawn, pessimistic client can be encouraged to recognize and accept the child, the parent, and the adult in himself, but particularly the child who is spontaneous and creative as well as willfully destructive and self-centered. "Would you kick a child for not running before he has learned to walk? So why push the child in you? Give him time to grow up." False dichotomies of thinking ("Either I am bad or good." "Either you agree with me or you don't love me.") are also pointed out to him. These polarities represent demands for unconditional acceptance of his ideas, behavior or moods, no matter how antisocial or destructive they are.

How does a client know that he has changed? Only when he knows the difference between the child who, feeling himself a victim, blames others and the adult who assumes full responsibility for everything he does. And only when he, not the therapist, has made a healthy decision to function on the socially useful side of life. For, as Nietzsche said, "The moment of choice is man's creative opportunity."

REFERENCES

1. Adler, A.: *Superiority and Social Interest.* Edited by H. L. and Rowena R. Ansbacher. Evanston, Ill., Northwestern University Press, 1964, pp. 96–111.
2. Dreikurs, R.: Psychotherapy as correction of faulty social values. *J Individ Psychol,* 13:150–158, 1957.
3. Spitzer, E. P.: Counseling aging persons with self-bounded life styles. *J Individ Psychol,* 22:104–111, 1966.

23

THE PROTESTING STUDENT

Arthur G. Nikelly

ADLER conceptualized individual behavior as, essentially, the product of man's interaction with his social environment. During the last half century this environment has changed drastically; consequently, the treatment of maladaptive behavior must adopt principles consistent with a new concept of man within his social environment. Increasing democratization requires new rules for living and adjusting, and the characteristics of maladjustment have come to differ from those prevalent during the earlier part of the century. Therapeutic techniques based on the autocratic philosophy of the past no longer prove effective, and treatment procedures must incorporate current democratic principles of living.

The decade of the sixties has been characterized by unrest and protest among secondary and college students; the unique and complex social and education problems to which these students are reacting require special effort to understand. This phenomenon of dissent is manifested in students who try to change the undemocratic aspects of the academic system through direct involvement in it, and sometimes their aggression is out of proportion to the problem (activists), and in students who drop out entirely from the scene (hippies). In either case, these students are saying "No" to the academic establishment which they see as autocratic and unduly rigid. They provoke the establishment with unconventional attire, by consuming illegal drugs, and by declaring their admiration for Che and Mao. These students seldom seek therapy because of their dissenting views but may seek psychological assistance because of feelings of depression, anxiety, or apathy, or because of rejection by the opposite sex, conflict with parents, existential concerns, or insomnia. These adjustment problems, typical of the adolescent and the young adult, are generally of a transient nature and are often labeled as a crisis in "identity."

In order to understand the protesting student it is necessary to take into account the nature of the academic structure. Current education theory maintains that students are of equal value with adults, but in practice students are expected to follow standards established by the educational hierarchy and are treated as subordinates responsible to their superiors. It is this inconsistency to which students object, even though they may recognize that these conditions can work to their advantage in later life. Inequality with the adult world and exclusion from participation in the formation of the policies governing secondary and higher education make many students feel oppressed and deprived of the opportunity to make meaningful decisions for which they can be held accountable.[2] Consequently, they are dissatisfied in fulfilling endless requirements which they see as irrelevant to their needs and without correspondence to social reality.

Studies show a relationship between the type of academic structure and the degree of student unrest and protest. The more autocratic and authoritarian in its teaching and administrative attitude is the institution, the greater is the tendency of its students to become dissatisfied. Conversely, students are not apt to protest if the institution is liberal, nonrestrictive and supportive of their rights, and treats them on a relatively equal basis.[5] When educators and administrators are primarily interested in preserving their own status and in safeguarding conditions as they are, students feel useless, stifled, and forced into remaining dependent. Youthful rebellion has also been encouraged through the neglect of institutions in secondary and higher education to cultivate social feeling, an ingredient necessary to viable democratic processes. Instead, these institutions use autocratic methods to control students who study the philosophy of democracy in theory only. Flacks,[3] it is interesting to note, describes several themes in the thinking of protesting students which seem close to Adler's concept of social feeling: their interest in communal participation and in authentic human relationships, their search for a humanitarian morality and for community feeling, their antiauthoritarian attitude which refuses to compromise with coersive and unilateral decisions, and their belief in the ability of all persons to participate collectively in solving problems as opposed to decisions by the elite. Although protesting students as a group are not homogeneous, the counselor would do well to bear these ideas in mind when dealing with the problems of an individual dissenting student. He should be aware that these students are accustomed to an environment which encourages the meshing of disparate viewpoints for the rational solution of human problems.

Adler's approach to the education of children and young adults is most appropriate in this time of student unrest and is founded on the premise that authentic personal freedom will develop only as the individual learns to maintain self-control and to respect order and the rights of others.[4] His concept of law and order, however, was built on democratic guidelines developed by the students themselves and based on their determining what is beneficial to everyone concerned rather than on the decisions of authority over which the students have no control. He felt that personal freedom can develop only in proportion to the degree of responsibility that the student is able to assume. This formula for guidance, so badly needed in our day, is consistent with the democratic philosophy which has been extolled in theory but seldom practiced by those in authority and by many adults in society who are expected to serve as models of good behavior for the young. Parents and educators want the young to become "critical," "self-reliant" and to "think for themselves," but when the latter try to become involved in the decision-making process of the school or university or point out the hypocrisy and inconsistent values of society, they are rejected and labeled "rebellious," "hostile" and "cynical." Students, consequently, may choose passive-aggressive behavior as the only response left for them. Parents and educators, in turn, try to overpower them with outdated and ineffective pedagogical methods and, thus, the battle between the generations continues.

Although many of the therapy techniques cited in previous chapters are applicable in guiding and reorienting the adolescent and young adult, the following specific recommendations will be helpful to the counselor or therapist in remotivating the rebelling student.

    1. Treat him with respect and on an equal basis, without the prejudice that he is inferior and unable to decide for himself. Let him know that what he says is worthwhile and that he has a

right to think for himself. The therapist must win the student's respect so that eventually he will be able to generalize positive feelings toward persons other than the therapist.

2. Avoid being shocked or repulsed by his appearance; he has the right to wear what he wants. Accept him on his own terms and for what he is. Avoid a power struggle, since the dissenting student is sensitive to authority and to anyone identified with the "system." Comparisons with more "normal" students will prevent him from benefiting from the therapeutic encounter. Condescension, cynicism, and hypocrisy will be immediately sensed by the student.

3. Do not regard him as a deviant or maladjusted person; maintain the assumption that he is basically a good person and that only his behavior or actions are annoying to many people. Consider him an adult, even though he is still an adolescent. Avoid excessive philosophical discussions or quibbling over controversial issues; such discussions often merely help the student to rationalize his unacceptable behavior and his negative stance toward the academic establishment. Share with him the notion that many of his feelings and ideas have been experienced by other persons who eventually found workable solutions without surrendering themselves to the system. Stress partial compromise as an available option.

4. Refrain from exploring personal matters with a passive-aggressive or negativistic student who has been referred because of antisocial behavior; such probing may put him on the defensive or cause him to think that he will be "brainwashed." In the initial sessions center the discussion on a neutral topic in which both student and counselor are reasonably versed. The therapist, for instance, may initiate a dialogue on architecture, athletics, or travel that brings them together until the student trusts the therapist and feels at home with him. As they get to know each other, the therapist can gradually shift the discussion to more relevant areas without causing the student to feel that he is being intimidated by the counselor to change his behavior.

5. Instead of focusing on the student's actions, the therapist must try to understand his motivation, that is, the story behind his actions. He should look for the message the student is giving

through his behavior. His actions are the logical outgrowth of his thinking; consequently, his behavior makes sense to him. From his own viewpoint his actions are "right."

6. Rather than interpreting the student's behavior directly, the usual procedure for many cases, the therapist may find that humor and anecdotes are more effective in conveying a message to the student. Adler[1] maintains that personal growth can be enhanced with wit and humor which introduce a new and valid point of view to the client. Anecdotes convey an alternate frame of reference, can throw new light on a baffling situation, and may reconcile the client to a different and more workable interpretation of a problem. Students in particular accept humor and anecdotes with a positive frame of mind because they feel the therapist is not trying to tamper with their personal lives.

7. It is often helpful to have the dissenting student describe exactly the situation to which he is reacting. Most rebellious students are honest and sensitive; in many instances their complaints are realistic and sincere, but they have difficulty communicating with others than their peers. The more they feel victimized, the greater their conflict with society becomes. Their reactions to a situation which they perceive as undesirable and stifling must be accepted by the counselor as a natural response and as a healthy attitude toward conditions which do not promote human growth and do not contribute to one's education. However, the crucial action for the counselor is to help the student discern whether his actions and feelings are in proportion to the situation which provoked them.

8. The protesting student can be encouraged through the counselor to communicate his ideas and to develop a dialogue with teachers and administrators who are willing to participate and to discuss issues. Arranging a conference between these groups might be appropriate, and the student can prove his usefulness by participating in decisions which affect himself and his school. It might well be remembered that during the period of Athenian democracy, students in the Lyceum and in other schools participated in making decisions governing their education and took a direct part in the administrative functions of the institution.

9. By emphasizing the consequences of the dissenting student's

actions, the counselor may help him to see how others are affected by his behavior. He can be encouraged to think of ways to carry out his liberal programs which will not alienate others. The student should be made aware of the possible consequences of alienation should he pursue an unrealistic course of action which cannot be achieved with the means at his disposal. Although he is free to do whatever he wants, he must be willing to accept the outcome of his actions and prepared to take responsibility for their consequences.

10. Finally, the student may be provided with alternatives regarding a course of action that may affect his life later. He can be allowed to draw his own conclusions after having examined these possibilities. The student should be helped to enlarge his views so that his decision will be based on a more complete and accurate picture of himself and his world. The more the counselor can demonstrate to the student that he understands a diversity of thinking, the better are the chances that the student will change his behavior.

REFERENCES

1. Adler, A.: *The Individual Psychology of Alfred Adler.* Edited by H. L. and Rowena R. Ansbacher. New York, Basic Books, 1956, p. 252.
2. Christensen, O. C.: The Student's Crusade Against Authority. In W. L. Pew (Ed.): *The War Between the Generations.* Minneapolis, Minnesota Society of Individual Psychology, 1968, pp. 12–16.
3. Flacks, R.: The liberated generation: An exploration of the roots of student protest. *J Soc Issues,* 23:52–75, 1967.
4. Furtmüller, C.: Alfred Adler: A Biographical Essay. In H. L. and Rowena R. Ansbacher (Eds.): *Superiority and Social Interest.* Evanston, Ill., Northwestern University Press, 1964, pp. 374–382.
5. Kenniston, K.: The sources of student dissent. *J Soc Issues,* 23:108–137, 1967.

24

DRUG ADDICTION

David Laskowitz

THE DESIRE TO TAKE medicine is probably among the salient features that distinguish man from his fellow creatures. Tranquilizers and antidepressants have, it is true, aligned the treatment of mental illness more closely to that of physical illness and have, thereby, contributed to an increased tolerance for mental and emotional disturbance. Unfortunately, however, a less desirable result has been society's enchantment with such drugs; we have found it easier to cope with life's problems by altering the internal environment than by struggling with external situations.

It is useful to study the addictive state with reference to Alfred Adler's basic construct of social interest. Adler [1] defined social interest as the capacity to understand and to accept one's social interrelatedness, to empathize with one's fellow man, to strive in a socially useful manner, and to concur with social realities. Addicts, clearly, come from heterogeneous life circumstances, reflect diverse lifestyles, and demonstrate wide variation in social interest.

Although individuals, depending on their state of mind and on the nature of stimuli from the social environment, respond differently to drugs, it remains true that there is generally a drug of choice. Persons, for example, who have not adopted an active motoric orientation, may seek sedatives rather than stimulants. The principle of drug choice obtains even in cases of multiple drug abuse, whether of the horizontal (drugs of different pharmacologic classes) or vertical (drugs of the same class) type. The discovery of a particular psychoactive drug with adaptive value will depend on whether the user is seeking oblivion, experiential stimulation, or personality change and is usually limited to the following four categories of pharmaca.

1. Sedative-hypnotic substances which include ethanol-containing drugs (whiskey, wine, beer), barbiturates, marijuana, and drugs formerly called "minor tranquilizers" such as meprobamate (Miltown®), chlordiazepoxide (Librium®), and diazepam (Valium®).

2. Opiate derivatives which include heroin, morphine, and narcotics synthetics.

3. Hallucinogenic (or dysleptic) drugs with selective central nervous system stimulating properties such as LSD-25, STP, mescaline, and psilocybin.

4. General central nervous system stimulants which include drugs of the amphetamine-type, nicotine and caffeine.

The oblivion seeker tends to seek cortical depressant drugs, especially the opiates, for their adjustive value. Since opiates elevate the threshold for the perception of threatening stimuli and suspend self-critical functions, their use provides a safeguard against feelings of inadequacy.

The search for oblivion is usually associated with the ghetto opiate addict who seeks to escape from conditions of human misery and hopelessness. He has, in the main, grown up in neglect and experiences his milieu as an enemy camp occupied by uncaring and untrustworthy persons where worth and power are measured by material acquisition. Having experienced repeated failure, he may adopt an ethic of "better me than you." Burdened by feelings of incompetence and despair in dealing with the three basic tasks of life—sexual, social, and occupational relations—he seeks chemical fortifiers.

The opiate user tends to withdraw from competition for women since sexual desire, for the most part, is conveniently dissolved with the use of the hypodermic needle. Since he may overvalue the masculine role and set conquest and acquisition as his sexual goals, the opiate addict can avoid the prospect of defeat and failure when "high." A subgroup of opiate addicts, on the other hand, derive a sense of heightened sexual competence because opiates enable them to maintain an erection and forestall ejaculation, even though achieving orgasm is difficult. If the addict is married, he may be unconcerned about his role as parent and provider when in an intoxicated state. Indeed, his ability to work at all or to share even a token amount of his income with his family is an achievement. If his lifestyle evolved from material and emotional neglect, he may only dimly envision what love and cooperation can be, since he is unprepared for these experiences by suitable role models. If his life pattern was based on the pampering attitude of others, he may hold an unrealistic sense of personal worth and expect to receive without giving and to rule others through his demands.

The drug experimenter often separates himself from nonusers in a desire to reaffirm his uniqueness and to enhance his self-esteem by being with the more "prestigious" drug-experimenting element of his peer group. Once involved in the addict subculture, he is increasingly alienated from nonusers. Soon his activity is totally directed to the socially "useless" side of life and his behavior becomes compulsively narcotics-centered. Whether or not an individual had developed social interest and social competence prior to addiction is often central to his response to treatment. If he began the use of narcotics early under extenuating circumstances (in response to peer pressure in a neighborhood where drug use is endemic), the prognosis is more hopeful than if he began drug use late in life in response to a psychiatric emergency. Similarly, the treatment outlook for a youngster whose drug use is embedded in a pattern of family value-violating behavior with little environmental pressure for drug experimentation is discouraging.

Effective occupational adjustment implies cooperation with others for a common benefit. The addict frequently sabotages his work situation by taking drugs. His problem in dealing with anger or, more precisely, with feelings of vulnerability may conflict with the authority of his boss and with the demands for cooperation of co-workers. The interpersonal substrate of the work situation and the attendant friction ultimately activate his doubts about his personal worth. Most jobs do not "turn him on," since they are experienced as menial and without a future. If he is a ghetto addict who began drug use at an early age, he has, in fact, little educational or vocational preparation for competing for more prestigious jobs. The temptation to shortcircuit the time and effort required for job training by selling drugs for a quick profit is great, even though as a user his profits are totally absorbed by "shooting up."

Perhaps the largest segment of oblivion-seekers using nonopiate substances such as marijuana or LSD belong to middle class, "dropout" culture. They view life as a game in which hypocritical roles are played according to rules set by an emotionally remote "establishment." Ambition and striving are seen as traps to ensnare the unsuspecting into organizing their lives around corrupt, long-term values instead of fulfilling present, more urgent needs. As an antidote to the hypocrisy of life they find an amotivational syndrome in which they forego achievement and disavow competition. Instead, they focus on the immediate and the unscheduled; they "hang out" and await a "happening" which may be an insightful experience pertaining to self or environment or merely an encounter with "beautiful people." Carey[2] notes that despite middle-class status of these oblivion seekers, they have little power, prestige, or access to the means of communication. Their disaffection comes from a sense of powerlessness and despair in being unable to reconstitute political and social structures in their own behalf. In Adlerian terms we are describing here a social interest that has become misdirected in the search for a more meaningful cultural ethos.

Paradoxically, the experience seeker may also rely on opiates. Although as cortical depressants, opiates have a generally constricting effect on awareness and obtund sensory impression, for some, they serve to facilitate behaviorial functions that are otherwise blocked by anticipatory anxiety. This facilitating effect may be observed in activities involving any of the three life tasks, that is, in social, sexual, and occupational performance. Apart from the facilitating influence associated with the pharmacologic action of opiates, many addicts are as "hooked" to the drug scene as they are to the drug itself. The life of the narcotics addict creates an illusion of involvement as he hustles around the clock and returns with harrowing tales of how he averted arrest and outmaneuvered "pushers." Such a life provides a deceptive sense of achievement and self-importance. For many addicts, if the need to acquire drugs was removed, there would be unbearable empty gaps to fill in their lives.

Most substances in the above four categories of drugs can help the addict find increasing accessibility to experience. The sedative-hypnotic group (alcohol and marijuana) in its disinhibiting phase may produce a sense of well-being, relieve fatigue, and enable the user to bear more cheerfully the strain and monotony of daily routine. Stimulants such as amphetamine-type and cocaine are clearly used for their antifatigue and antidepressant properties.

The dysleptic substances (LSD-25, DMT, STP, mescaline, psilocybin) are, however, the drugs most typically abused by experience seekers in the service of "expanding consciousness." The reasons usually cited for their use is that they enable the user to experience God or some other supernatural being in a new, more significant spiritual fashion. Such an experience presumably generates a sense of heightened inner strength and lessens the need to struggle with the complexities of the universe. In the course of the mystical experience, the user survives the loss of ego boundaries and feels at one with the universe. This fusion experience may be a resurgence of a wish for closeness and intimacy of an earlier developmental period. Interestingly, users do not move toward organized religion subsequent to this experience.

Another alleged motive for the use of dysleptic drugs is the experience of spontaneous social expression. Presumably, the user experiences heightened freedom in initiating personal contact. The supposed spill-over from increased social to physical intimacy may have contributed to the aphrodisiac mystique of LSD. The social interest stimulated by the use of dysleptics is, however, usually short-lived.

A third reason for using dysleptic drugs is the subsequent improvement in aesthetic ability cited by artists or would-be artists. The heightening of creative powers is a transient condition for those without previous experience in aesthetic undertakings who discover their artistic talents for the first time while under the influence of drugs. Perhaps truly gifted persons are better able to integrate the perceptions and thoughts aroused by LSD, but in both instances, the goal of superiority through augmented artistic powers is usually elusive.

As Rene Dubos [3] points out, the *normal* personality maintains an orderly and integrated response to stimuli given by normal life. Interference with this response by psychoactive agents can have a disintegrative effect on personality; however, in the case of abnormal personality structures, e.g. borderline schizophrenics, substances such as opiates can have a restitutive function and may forestall decompensation under the unremitting impact of stress. One must, therefore, distinguish between the use of drugs as pharmacological help in providing symptomatic relief and the use of drugs for personality change. It is known, for example, that opiates, by attenuating anger or sexual feelings, have adaptational value for many. Similarly, users of hypnotic-sedative substances such as marijuana or alcohol may seek relief from socially induced anxiety and become more responsive to their surroundings.

The desire for personality change is, however, primarily associated with the user of dysleptic substances, notably LSD-25. Indeed, this substance has been used in the treatment of alcoholics and a variety of other psychiatric entities with variable results. The user of dysleptic drugs strives for power in the intellectual and the social spheres. His search for heightened mental capacity is reflected in increased empathic and intellectual skills and in new insights into his lifestyle. He maintains an expectation of instant Zen. In the social sphere, he seeks to experience greater love for his fellow man, a goal frequently reported by persons who have been loners or hostile. If improved interpersonal relations and social warmth are experienced, they are rarely sustained. Once again, the drug user attempts to acquire social feelings in an effortless, chemical way.

Typically, the addict begins treatment without motivation, unless the treatment modality is chemically-oriented, viz. methadone maintenance or cyclazocine (an opiate-antagonist). Reasons for seeking treatment may range from the desire to detoxify and recuperate physically because maintenance of the habit (in terms of cost or quantity) has become unmanageable to the necessity for finding a place to stay or the means for warding off court action. The addict enters treatment intending to perpetuate his mistaken lifestyle and is not interested in being helped to do the things within his power.

The therapist cannot rely on ordinary conversation in getting to know the addict. Language is essentially a social product, and the addict has long since challenged or repudiated the validity of societal norms. Often he will engage in barren small-talk or will lie openly. Free association is rarely effective, for this technique is too abstract and unstructured for the addict who fundamentally distrusts a task involving a chain of ideas without a predetermined goal. A task that cannot be "sized-up" is potentially unsafe. Useful information can be obtained, however, from concrete verbal tasks that minimize probing connotations—the telling of early recollections, an account of "real" things such as the day's experience in the street, at home, or on the job. Excessive attention to narcotics-centered anecdotes is to be avoided, since this dialogue promotes a sense of importance to the drug user as he diverts the therapist's attention.

Treatment must be holistic and deal with the addict's interactions within his ecological unit (his family and neighborhood). Since the therapist's most reliable ally is the client himself and his capacity for self-observation, the opiates which suspend self-criticism must be withdrawn. Although nonchemical treatment approaches which remove the hard-core addict from his drug-use surroundings are desirable and, indeed, often necessary, they rarely effect a change in lifestyle. Geographic "cures" are seldom maintained. The client needs an introduction to a new way of life which often cannot be provided by out-patient therapy. Therapy in residence can be conducive to life goal change by providing a sustained challenge to the addict's flight from social feeling and social responsibility. Ex-addicts may serve as models which check the addict's pessimistic predictions about his future; professional staff can assist in the task of explaining the addict to himself.

Addicts are likely to have a "hidden agenda," an essential but latent communication which must be extricated from their manifest productions. The therapist must, however, use an analytic, uncovering approach with caution and avoid giving the impression that he is more interested in the treatment process than in the client. A synthesizing approach wherein the therapist helps the client find, in the seemingly discordant data of his life, the unifying thread that clearly demonstrates his hidden, largely unconscious, goal-orientation is well suited to the treatment of the addict. The therapist must skillfully translate this information into emotionally incisive language without making the client feel humiliated or condemned. Moralizing, upbraiding, and the citing of catchy slogans such as "crime is a coward's imitation of heroism," are unlikely to be of value. Ideally, confirmation of the therapist's understanding should reside in the content of the concrete event that the addict chooses to discuss. The formulation of the lifestyle should come from the addict and not be imposed upon him. Similarly, he frequently resents the so-called "focused question" that implies its answer. Because addicts often have fantasies of omnipotence, though these may be well masked, the therapist will gain respect if he can make astute predictions regarding the addict's course of action. Therapy progresses as the reality basis of the therapist's views is established in contrast to his magical powers or to the addict's apperceptive distortions.

Only when the client perceives the therapist as reliable, consistent, and straightforward will he accept his interpretations. Since the addict enters treatment with a distrust of authority, he readily distinguishes between honest expression and the oblique sophistry of the therapist who hides behind language. The therapist must avoid self-conscious efforts to build a positive relationship with the addict. An initial maneuver which is frequently effective in dealing with a "hardened" adolescent is to undermine his fantasy that he is a colorful desperado by relating to him in an interested, professional manner. It is often difficult to react sympathetically to addicts who seem to enjoy their symptoms in the face of society's disapproval; whereas it is easier to show compassion for neurotics who are manifestly experiencing psychological pain. On the other hand, the therapist must not reinforce the addict's misconception of himself as a person who, by the mere fact of his existence, is of extraordinary value to others. The beginning therapist may unwittingly promote this fiction by creating a "rescue fantasy" in which he shores up his own sense of significance by endeavoring to have an impact on the addict at all costs.

One way to disturb the addict's magical beliefs is to call him to account for infractions of ground rules, regardless of how negligible they may seem or whether they pertain to the conditions of the treatment contract in individual or group therapy, or to the house rules of a residence. Addicts frequently have gotten away with petty offenses or, when caught, manipulated others by "making deals" or seducing them to delinquency. When devoid of hostility, such calling to account is a valuable treatment experience. The therapist must demonstrate to the addict that his interests are actually identical to those of society and are therefore best served when his behavior is socially constructive.

Addicts usually desire to rule, and this manipulative desire must be controlled. Realistic controls are, however, not punitive, just as permissiveness is not necessarily therapeutic. Addicts will initially test the therapist severely: How gullible is he? Will he get angry if the addict is absent for several sessions? To what extent can the therapist be subjugated by tears and complaints? The therapist soon learns that any commitments he makes can be used to defeat him. Though limits are part of social reality, the way limits are set by the therapist and interpreted by the addict determines whether a power struggle will be incited. Frequently the addict tests the therapist by provoking him to anger. When the therapist's actions are construed by the client as punishment, the latter considers them to be an affirmation of his war with society and is challenged to circumvent the punishment. However, if the therapist allows the addict to suffer the natural consequences of his actions, without humiliating him, the experience may prove effective.

The client may try to limit the therapist's freedom of action through explicit, direct maneuvers or through implicit, indirect approaches. Both ways retain the initiative for the client though they are self-defeating. Among the direct maneuvers used by the addict are the following:

1. The client may exhibit demanding behavior ranging from an urgent insistence that the therapist be available whenever needed to infinite requests for services, many of which have just enough relevance to be reasonable. The client may also insist on a variety of medications to enable him to function more effectively; he may even specify the sedatives required and the dose level.

2. The client may attempt to set conditions for therapy. The therapist must explain that this behavior reflects the client's need to be buttressed by special considerations; presumably his feelings of vulnerability are greater than those of his peers who do not need this advantage. When such behavior occurs in a Residence or in group therapy, the therapist may point out his equal responsibility to all and appeal to the client's group loyalty.

3. The client with after-care status may endeavor to substitute a phone call for a treatment session. When this happens, the therapist must explore the basis for the addict's resistance. Among the indirect maneuvers are the following: 1) self-depreciation and manipulation of the therapist's sympathy, 2) an expression of hurt, surprise, or disappointment in treatment results in order to put the therapist on the defensive or to render him impotent, 3) "quoting" other staff members in contradistinction to the therapist's views as a wedging operation whereby the addict hopes to maintain control by promoting inconsistent behavior from the therapist.

Unless the nonopiate user is in a disequilibrate state, e.g. after a bad LSD trip, motivation for treatment is usually low. Precisely because he is not using "hard narcotics," he is less likely to concede that he has a serious drug problem, and abstinence from chemicals cannot always be made a precondition for therapy. As with the opiate addict, the therapeutic intent is to transform the user into a patient. The therapist's dilemma is that the user is probably from the middle class, articulate, adept at psychologizing, and harbors a mistrust of the therapist's "establishment," "over thirty" attitudes. He has already repudiated his family's value system and his drug use has probably forced them to "sit up and take notice." He may consider himself to be an individual by virtue of his pervasive renunciations; he is proudly classless, homeless, moneyless, and schoolless.

A frequent ploy of the user, especially of hallucinogens, is, "How can you help me if you have never turned on?" This argument is the mirror image of the parental behavior from which they purport to have "cut loose," for they frequently complain that the only way they can get together with their parents is to capitulate to the latter's standards. The therapist can, of course, invoke the analogy that one does not have to be schizophrenic to work with schizophrenics. It is ironic that the non-opiate user has taken one of the Establishment's favorite agents, drugs, in his attempt to dissociate himself from that Establishment.

Since chemical users are not a homogeneous group, it is important to understand the specific adaptive value of the chemical taken, the way each individual benefits from the substance used. Recourse to chemicals may be a misdirected route toward experiencing social interest. The therapist must convey effectively the attitude that "We are all in this together, that having created social reality we are capable of changing it." As with the opiate addict, the therapist must teach the chemical user to reach out on a human level, to modify his lifestyle through socially useful activity. The therapist may focus on conscious productions and on the manifest content of dreams, not as screens behind which real meaning lies, but to help the client understand the "script" that he produces, directs, and enacts. The client must grasp the world that he constructs in terms of time, space and causality. If he is to relinquish the socially corrosive delusion that the way to live is to drop out, if he is to stop seeing the present solely through the past and become accessible to the liberating possibilities of the future, the therapist must demonstrate how freedom of choice is blocked by safeguarding attitudes which promote the *status quo*. The process of "turning on" to oneself is clearly the antidote to the seductive thesis of "better living through chemistry" and may, in fact, prepare the drug user for survival.

REFERENCES

1. Adler, A.: *Superiority and Social Interest.* Edited by H. L. and Rowena R. Ansbacher. Evanston, Ill.: Northwestern University Press, 1964, pp. 29–40.
2. Carey, J.: Marijuana use among the new bohemians, In P. E. Smith (Ed.): *J Psychedelic Drugs,* 2:79–93 (Issue I). San Francisco, Calif., Haight-Ashbury Medical Clinic, 1968.
3. Dubos, R.: On the Present Limitation of Drug Research. In P. Talalay (Ed.): *Drugs in Our Society.* Baltimore, Md., Johns Hopkins Press, 1964, p. 86.

25

DELINQUENCY

Ernst Papanek

THE YOUTH OF TODAY are not less disoriented than their elders who are frightened by hydrogen bombs and economic and social insecurity. When endangered in life and spirit by a bewildered and frightened society, they become a danger, bewildering and frightening to others.

Our society, after suffering seriously from the destructive behavior of its deviates, has reacted violently against them. It has built countless legal barriers, courts, punishment, prisons, reformatories; and yet efforts to protect society by these means and the remedies to prevent recurrence of destructive activities have proved unsatisfactory and inefficient. They practically have failed. As long as only the criminal act was considered, and not the actor and the reasons why he acted that way, no promising tool was found and developed in the fight against crime and delinquency.

There are, of course, many causes of juvenile delinquency, as well as many methods and cures for it. Whether it is sickness or sin, or just a symptom of an emotional disturbance to which the delinquent was predisposed or which he acquired; whether parents or teachers are the more responsible; whether it is a case of bad company or bad character —in any event, juvenile delinquency must never be regarded only as a psychological but always as a social deviation. Otherwise it is not juvenile delinquency. The treatment that does not face this fact must inevitably fail. The legal definition is irrelevant regarding the mere psychiatric aspects of the problem, but certainly it is not irrelevant to the social aspects, since it strongly affects the treatment given.

Juvenile delinquency is rarely the product of biological sickness. As a purposeful reaction, it springs more often from a frustrated or deficient, immature mind—a mind that will not see alternatives to obtaining, in deviate ways, the needed self-preservation, acceptance, friendship, and love. Our treatment must show the young deviate that there is another alternative, a better one, that we can help him find and use, more efficient, less anxious and, therefore, more successful ways to achieve these ends.

A child confronted by an abnormal situation feels lost, insecure, upset, aggressive. If he finds no help in trying to meet the situation, he may become a delinquent. Most such children have experienced frustration, insecurity, anxiety and tension, and often explode into aggressive, antisocial behavior. Unguided guilt feelings following such behavior provoke still more insecurity, greater anxiety and tension, which again explode into vengefulness due to this hopelessness and frustration. We must interrupt this "vicious circle."

Children who have never known understanding, love, prestige, social acceptance, or who have misinterpreted or misused these feelings when offered in an overprotective and unchallenging way, do not need punishment. Punishment will only intensify the frustration which produces this pattern of disturbance and delinquency, and only teaches the child how to punish. By showing him that we understand, we teach him understanding; by helping him, we teach him to help; by cooperating, we teach him to cooperate.

We do not treat just the particular crime that has been committed, for we are not interested in a single, behavioral expression. It is our job to consider the whole personality, the delinquent aspect and its nondelinquent counterpart. There are many phases of normal and seminormal adolescent behavior to be considered, as well as the partially pathological, half-pathological and wholly pathological, psychopathological and sociopathological behavior patterns. This is why we are so often flabbergasted by the different attitudes in children living in what is allegedly the same environment. The fact is, that environment is never the same, since in a family with two children, for instance, the parents' favoritism for one child may easily mean normal development for one and delinquent development for the other.

Some other controversial factors to think about: We are used to delinquency springing from poverty and deprivation, and we are therefore surprised to encounter delinquency due to affluence and overabundance, forgetting that overabundance may amount simply to deprivation of challenge. There is delinquency due to urbanization, but it also exists where young people want and need to escape a rural existence in response to the lure of glamorous city life.

From Alfred Adler we learn that harmonious life must consider successful relationship to society, work, and love, with all three closely interwoven. Its motivations are not mysterious drives or instincts, but logical needs of communal living. The way to improvement lies not in repressions or sublimations, but in increasing the cooperative and social abilities.[1]

The entire community is responsible for delinquency. Since parents are close to children, more responsibility, of course, can be traced to them, but schools, churches and synagogues, the lack of recreational facilities, and especially the reactions of the community to crime and criminals, to comics, movies, television, and radio are also involved in the problem. The ill-defined status of our youth in society, their feeling that they have no role in it, also contributes to juvenile delinquency.

We must convince the child that we do not demand blind obedience or timid adherence to rules and regulations, to thoughts and behavior he does not understand. We want him to learn, by example, by doing, and by living, that the "iron laws of human co-living" make it impossible for any individual to achieve security or happiness, acceptance, prestige, friendship, or love, if his actions do not contribute to the well-being of the other members of his society.

All environmental and psychological factors are therapeutically important. Successful treatment of a juvenile delinquent often requires treatment not only of the delinquent but also of his parents, teachers, siblings, his entire environment. Consequently, a true reorientation of all the educational factors involved is needed. The least we must do in such cases is obtain the cooperation of all of these. Where we cannot, we have to provide substitutes that will cooperate or will help us make the others do so. Child guidance workers must therefore work simultaneously with parents and teachers, and for the socially handicapped delinquent, we must provide probation officers who will give adequate supervision while enforcing treatment needs. In still other cases, we must provide institutional care, so that the child's entire environment is changed in the interests of more efficient treatment.

In the process of education and treatment—whether in a child guidance clinic, parole, probation, or institutional setting—understanding and "permissiveness" are only the first step, a preliminary stage. Reorientation and reeducation will often dictate that the child experiences the consequences of his own actions. Such consequences are beneficial only if they dramatize the problem to the child, and if he is given constructive help in facing these consequences. There is, at most, a negligible danger that such an offer of help will be abused or misinterpreted, whereas deliverance from anxiety and tension may almost always be expected in the "offender." These are the best bases for treatment and constructive education. Friendly help and example can aid the child to better understand what makes his behavior intolerable to society, how to avoid trouble, and the way to live an individual life that is happier and more socially constructive.

The immediate treatment goal is to make the child accessible to reeducation by lessening his inferiority feeling and anxieties, by relieving his tensions—created by hostile social pressure—by decreasing his hostile and destructive behavior, and by removing internal and external causes of his emotional disturbance.

Confidence in the therapist or educator, based on fair treatment and not simply on so-called transference, can give the juvenile delinquent a sense of security among his peers and adults. This confidence helps him establish an awareness and acceptance of the community, and will help him to understand and accept consequential behavior in social living.

"Consequences" are closely connected with the concept of responsibility. Legal responsibility for delinquent acts of a sick juvenile mind should, of course, be abolished. But we are wrong if we believe that the abolition of legal responsibility also means abolition of educational and psychological responsibility. The latter is necessary for all interpersonal human relationships. No treatment, no reeducation and in fact no education or growth can be achieved without it. The feeling of self-respect, of belonging, social feelings for other human beings—these are all meaningless if they are not closely connected with and not derived from and expressed in social and psychological responsibility.

Anything that fails to satisfy the need for esteem and self-actualization must leave the juvenile delinquent with the conviction that he remains inferior to his fellowmen. Under professional guidance, in a moderately challenging environment, engaging in trial and error without fear of frustration or failure, the delinquent can be helped to achieve that goal. There will be cases where it is impossible to make use of the normal environment, the community and the family in which the youngster became delinquent, cases where neither the child guidance clinic in school nor a special clinic nor probation will be able to provide such an environment, and we shall have to apply healing methods that would otherwise not be considered wholesome—the institutional situation. Such residential treatment has its own structure and dynamics and should not imitate the family, hospital or boarding school, or any other kind of children's institution. It is not a substitute for something else; it is the right instrument for helping the kind of children it serves. It therefore tries to provide a healing environment which at the same time enables the child to acquire new insight, a new outlook, new motivation, a better education, experience by trial and error, and practice in healthy and constructive living before returning to his normal social surroundings.

In the mind of the average person there is a sort of hierarchy of severity in the assignment of a deviate child to a child guidance clinic, probation, parole, foster parents, semi-liberty hostel, or institutional care. From the point of view of treatment, each of these assignments is simply the appropriate setting for the specific treatment required in a particular case. All should start their work on the same premise; therapeutically necessary prevention of a repetition of the delinquent acts. It is extremely important that the person fully grasps the fact that he is receiving not punishment but therapy, and that prevention is a vital first step in the treatment.

In a great percentage of children who get into trouble, we find that feeling guilty and ashamed because they had failed in school had not only made them truant but also defensive and hostile toward a society which demanded the knowledge of the three "R's" but had not helped them to acquire it. Relief from this emotional pressure will often come from remedial help by an expert teacher, rather than from psychotherapy.

It is important to develop in our children an appropriate desire for order, companionship and spontaneous social cooperation, as well as a love of fair play. This can be achieved only by untiring explanation and guidance, by practical demonstrations arranged in cooperation with the children themselves, and by having children really participate in the affairs of the community of which they are a part.

A society no longer willing to regard these children as expendable, whether their handicaps stem from social disorder or physical or emotional illness; a society interested in salvaging such children and making them assets to their communities instead of burdens—such a society must seek a better way to handle them, must endeavor to do a better job.

Recognizing all this, Adlerian psychology aids in the effective prevention of juvenile delinquency and in its reeducation and treatment with its concept of a practical philosophy for living:

1. To gain insight into human behavior by understanding it as a dynamic process of compensation for inferiority feelings.
2. To direct one's own striving and that of others toward the goal of social usefulness.
3. To strive for a goal of life and for immediate compensation in security for the individual in his society.
4. To help find the best way for developing man's creative abilities, to enable him to make his own choice and his own combination of choices in accordance with his inheritance and environments.

Any special aspects of treatment and reeducation of the juvenile delinquent, whether by child guidance, probation, parole, or institution consist mainly of showing him, interpreting for him, making him understand, accept and respect the role and function of others and himself in society. The goal is socialization and responsible cooperation, not submission and blind obedience. There is no need to achieve this by painful experience, but there is also not always a possibility or a need to make it all just fun. A feeling of security, however, a sense of belonging, responsibility, and satisfaction, are needed to serve as the basis for social and emotional dynamics and for constructive motivations.

Treatment of the juvenile delinquent, which is reeducation of an emotional and social deviate, must give him a new orientation, new incentives, inner controls; it must promote socially constructive motivations which will be rewarded by inner gratification and satisfaction, and it will have to diminish his fears and social anxieties, his inferiority feelings, depressions, and hostilities, while encouraging him to make positive and constructive decisions in human and social relations.[2]

REFERENCES

1. Adler, A.: *The Science of Living.* Edited by H. L. Ansbacher. New York, Doubleday, 1969, pp. 104–112.
2. Adler, A.: *Superiority and Social Interest.* Edited by H. L. and Rowena R. Ansbacher. Evanston, Ill., Northwestern University Press, 1964, pp. 253–268.

26

SUICIDE

Arthur G. Nikelly and Bertram P. Karon

Suicide is an alarming health and social problem and, despite its multiple motivational factors and demographic correlates, primarily represents a strong conflict between the individual and society. Suicide may function as an appeal for help or as an attempt at aggressive retaliation or both. Many times the individual is unaware of or ambiguous about his suicidal motivations and the reasons he offers cannot be taken at face value.

Usually those who have committed or attempted suicide indicated their intentions. Suicide may represent a solution to the person who feels emotionally rootless, lacks identity, and has no feeling of belonging. Those who attempt suicide usually resent others or are ambivalent in their feelings toward them; their suicide attempt represents an effort to change their relationship with others. A lack of verbal communication may often be the precursor of a suicidal attempt as well as its result. The act itself is nonverbal, and serves as a signal that the person is in deep distress.

The person who attempts or threatens suicide may be expressing hostility and aggression toward those with whom he interacts or appealing for their help. The validity of this statement is attested to the guilt a suicide attempt creates in others who may consequently place themselves in the service of the person who threatens suicide. The therapist must understand that such an appeal or threat, or both, is always implicit in the suicide attempt, although the person trying to commit suicide may not be aware of either function of his actions.

Therapy with such persons is predicated upon a very warm relationship that generates genuine rapport. As Kurt Adler [2] proposes, the therapist ought to "esteem the patient despite his negativism . . . despite his shabby devices, despite the malevolence he has shown to his relatives *and* to the therapist; when it can be shown that these actions were based on childhood errors that can be corrected in the present, and that there is hope for him to become a social human being; then, and only then, will cooperation with the therapist begin." If the person is overtly psychotic, manifests bizarre behavior, mental disorientation, and peculiar thinking, and does not sufficiently respond to psychotherapeutic intervention, hospitalization is a resource which can be and should be used to gain time. Since most nonlethal suicidal attempts are "messages" for attention, they can be interpreted as indications of a lack of genuine social interest, as evidence of self-centeredness and low self-esteem, and as an example of a hostile attitude toward a world which is not responding to narcissistic and self-centered needs. Basic dependency is invariably present and should be explored with the therapist, who should provide avenues through which the client can reevaluate himself and his actions, can be encouraged to reach out and can exhibit social thrust without fear of rejection. The client must be provided with opportunities to develop stronger social interest.

While depression is frequently found in suicidal acts, such acts should also be considered as aggressive, manipulative, and challenging gestures toward others who may not have returned affection or succumbed to the client's emotional needs. In controlling others by trying to hurt himself, he exhibits a deep feeling of isolation and the inability to accept life's stresses and disappointments. This lifestyle of dependency or defiance may be at the very basis of the suicidal intention, and the therapist should explore what meaning these stresses have upon the client. This examination can expose the client's misguided attitudes toward life and himself and his erroneous beliefs and thoughts which may be at the root of his desire to escape by suicide. He can intervene by helping the client determine the real source of his anger. He can help the client express his feelings legitimately through an interpersonal confrontation rather than by self-destruction and he can guide the client in questioning the effectiveness of suicide as a retaliatory gesture.

The therapist should consider a suicide threat as a movement by the client, since it invariably affects others around him, which may be one of the primary motives for performing such an act. In addition to trying to understand the situations and convictions which cause the individual to act in such a manner, the therapist should initiate a phase in which planning is structured with the client to provide hope, encouragement, insight, and support. The therapist should concentrate on eliciting the individual's distorted evaluation of himself and others and on encouraging him to identify and verbalize his aggressive tendencies as well as the purposes he feels they serve.

Suicide can be considered a retaliatory and aggressive act against important persons in the client's life or toward fantasies of significant figures in his past. Through suicide he feels he can hurt others by making them feel guilty and anguished. The therapist can directly contradict this fantasy (private logic) by stressing that others will not necessarily experience guilt as the result of his action; in fact, the more justified the client's anger, the less effective suicide will be as retaliation. "Denial of the effectiveness of suicide as a technique of retaliation, when combined with a warm therapeutic relationship that arouses in the patient a hope which cannot be realized in death, suffices to end the suicidal danger." [4]

Alfred Adler [1] first described the therapeutic technique of undercutting the client's fantasy of the effectiveness of suicide as a hostile gesture by arousing hope in his client. An example of this technique follows.

A female outpatient, age thirty-two, denied any suicidal ideas at the beginning of psychotherapy, despite projective tests which indicated a strong impulse toward suicide which was not entirely ego-syntonic. Six weeks later, when faced with an apparent breakup of her marriage, she telephoned one of the authors to tell him that she was about to kill herself. This was immediately interpreted as retaliation: "There's only one reason anyone kills herself. It's to get even with someone else. But it won't really hurt your husband. It'll just solve his problems for him. No indecision, and it will save him the price of a divorce. As for your parents, they will be glad to get rid of you. And I'll just get another patient."

The client became angry and insisted: "I am not trying to get even with anyone. I just feel hopeless. That's the stupidest interpretation I ever heard of. It has nothing to do with me."

Nevertheless, she did not kill herself. Further, she complained in later therapy session: "It wasn't true. It has nothing to do with me. But now I can't kill myself. I used to think that if things go too bad I could always kill myself. But now you've taken that possibility away from me."

Projective tests administered four months later showed that her suicidal impulses at that time were minimal.

Ansbacher [3] points out that the suicidal person is attempting to hurt others by causing injury to himself and trying to gain an advantage over them while taking no responsibility for his action. He cites the case of a young girl who respected her parents and felt close to them but wanted to commit suicide because of an "immoral" escapade. When confronted with the question of whether her parents would prefer a "bad" daughter or a dead daughter, her suicidal intentions dissipated.

Thus, the therapist may treat the suicidal person by destroying his illusions about death and by challenging his belief in his alleged effectiveness of suicide as a revengeful act. He may point out to him that people—including the therapist—will carry on their work, and that no one will react to his death as the client may expect. Above all, the therapist is expected to provide the suicidal client with a strong dose of social feeling and hopefulness, and to release his potential for becoming a useful member of society.

REFERENCES

1. Adler, A.: *Superiority and Social Interest*. Edited by H. L. and Rowena R. Ansbacher. Evanston, Ill., Northwestern University Press, 1964, pp. 239–252.
2. Adler, K. A.: Depression in the light of individual psychology. *J Individ Psychol*, 17:56–67, 1961.
3. Ansbacher, H. L.: Suicide as communication: Adler's Concept and Current Applications." *J Individ Psychol*, 25:174–180, 1969.
4. Karon, B. P.: Suicidal tendency as the wish to hurt someone else and resulting treatment technique. *J Individ Psychol*, 20:206–212, 1964.

Part VI   Educational
                 Techniques

27

THE CULTIVATION OF RESPONSIBILITY AND SELF-DISCIPLINE

MABELLE H. BROOKS

THE DEMOCRATIZATION of the family and society places greater emphasis on inner controls; consequently, education toward self-discipline and in the direction of social interest should begin early in life, at home and in the school. Adler firmly believed that maladjustment in later life could be significantly curtailed if educational measures were systematically applied by teachers early in the child's life so that he would be prepared to meet the tasks of adulthood.[1] He believed that the school—not society—is the child's best teacher, provided that it developed his potential for social interest and helped him to exercise freedom with an equal amount of responsibility.[2] The role of the counselor or teacher in the development of self-discipline and in the progressive maturation of children, adolescents, or adults is to correct faulty attitudes and habitual errors in behavior or, even more appropriately in the case of children, to keep these from occurring. Self-discipline is the development in the individual of attitudes and methods which make him able to solve problems and to meet new situations in ways beneficial to himself and to others.[5] Most of the following discussion involves work with children, but the idea can be adapted to the treatment of older persons.

The counselor or teacher must work like the gardener and first prepare the soil. *Interrelationship* is the basic idea to be established. Discussion begins with children about the number of homes they have. From their knowledge of a personal home, they progress to the idea of a village, town or city home and then to the concept of their country and the world as home. Children are invariably interested in maps and globes and will enjoy locating these various homes. During globe work, the teacher may demonstrate how our world continually turns without stopping—there is no place to get off. We can't have a pleasant world home, town home, or personal home unless we learn how to get along together. Next, the members of the family to which the child belongs are discussed: the father's tasks, the mother's tasks, and the part each child plays in family life as he grows up. To demonstrate the way parts make a strong whole, the children may make a cord by weaving pieces of string together. Singly each piece of string is weak and easily broken, but when they are woven together, no child can break the cord. In another illustration, ask each child to lift his dictionary with one finger, then with two, and then with the whole hand. Even the little finger helps in accomplishing the task. In extending this idea of interrelationship to the classroom, the teacher may initiate a valuable discussion stemming from an old rhyme which appeals to children.

> "What kind of a class would your class be,
> If every pupil were just like me?"

The second basic concept to be developed in cultivating responsibility is *self-worth* or *self-value*. Just as the little finger is important to the hand, so is each organ and member of use to the body. Similarly, each child, even the smallest, is part of the whole family. Each has his place to fill, his needs to be met, and his contribution to make. Each has value because he helps to make up the whole. In a similar fashion each family has a place in the great human family and a contribution to make. Once these ideas are thoroughly "mixed into the soil," they must be kept viable through casual and frequent reference. Then comes the planting of seeds—seeds we hope will lead to effective functioning of bodies, brains, and feelings.

Seed one is *preparation to meet discouragement.* Going to the piano, the teacher illustrates the Law of Learning by playing the scale. It is customary to begin any new task with enthusiasm, and we often do so well that we surprise ourselves. But when we come to the half-step in the scale, the teacher explains that this is called a "plateau." At this time our work slows down and we seem to be making no progress at all; however, we pass the plateau and go on to more whole steps. The secret of learning is to be prepared for the plateau, to accept it in stride, and to know that we will soon pass it by.

Handling mistakes is our second seed. A chance to plant this seed comes whenever one child laughs at another's mistake or is crestfallen over his own. Class work stops and mistakes are talked about. The teacher tells of mistakes she has made, and children think of many to add. Then she develops the idea that mistakes can be our friends; they show us where we need more help to understand or more practice in developing skills. If a mistake is made under circumstances which greatly embarrass us, we never forget it; we may work hard to prevent such a mistake from ever happening again, or we may give up and never try that task again. If we give up, we become a partial cripple. A stick figure can be used to represent this situation to children. Individual children may enjoy copying this figure in their notebooks. When a child becomes better at a task, he may lengthen the short leg, indicated by a dotted line. As he improves even more, the leg is finally drawn full length.

Seed three is the *way to tackle jobs*. The child is taught to check himself on the three parts of every job: 1) getting ready (tools out and work space arranged), 2) doing the task, 3) putting things away. Since everything in nature evolves by a certain pattern or rhythm, we can help the child to think about the pattern or rhythm by which he works best. Children enjoy noting earth rhythms such as day and night, the seasons, moon patterns, and the tides. They also notice the rhythms of their own bodies—inhaling, exhaling, pulse, and heart beat. Whenever the class appears fatigued or tense, rhythm to music refreshes and invigorates.

Self-measurement is a fourth seed. A useful yardstick is the question, "Is my act, my idea or my desire on the useful or useless side of life?" Even a young child can understand this. When report card time comes around, each child is asked to evaluate himself in each subject, on his class helpfulness, on his ability to get along with his classmates, on his efforts in general. He is asked in what ways he is especially eager to improve in skills or attitudes. His own evaluation is returned to him when he is given the teacher's report card. A bulletin board may be set aside where each child may share the paper or product of work which he prizes most during the week. A great effort is made to keep down comparisons which belittle any child and the emphasis is placed on the great variety of areas in which skills may lie. Every child can make his special contribution.

The fifth and last seed that we consciously plant is the *application of logical consequences*. Since our aim is to teach the child to take responsibility for his own acts, our recurrent question, after something is spilled or broken, is "What do you think you should do about it?" Most children quite naturally will offer to clean it up, to mend it, to pay for it, to work it out. If these solutions do not occur to a particular child, other pupils will soon make them obvious to him. In the matter of fights, particularly when combatants are unevenly matched, the teacher must stop the conflict. Sending the two to an empty room away from an audience usually enables them to work out a satisfactory settlement verbally, but they are always reminded that they may call on the teacher for her views if they need help.

The author, in developing a climate for personality growth and in building social feeling, has developed the following principles: [3]

1. Make each child feel that he is important to the group, that his help with work is needed, that his ideas are worth considering in connection with class problems, and that his participation in class activities is vital to all.

2. Praise effort involved rather than actual achievement. Get beneath surface talents and respond to the slow, discouraged child as well as to the quick, show-off or talented youngster.

3. Avoid all mention of "good," "bad," "better," "best" in characterizing children or their behavior.

4. Never fight verbally (or physically, of course) with a child. Maintain an attitude of good will—an expectation that the child wants to do his part. In the case of a child who refuses, recognize that we cannot meet the difficulty with force but must work it out matter-of-factly through natural consequences or through mutual agreement after discussion.

5. Never humiliate a child in private or in a group.

It goes without saying that even with the right soil and productive seeds the growth climate needed for children will not be provided unless the teacher or counselor is a mature person. He must like himself, not because he considers himself perfect, but because he feels himself a needed part of the human race. Genuine self-respect carries with it a certain dignity, whether he is dealing with a child, an adolescent, or an adult. In addition to a skilled, mature teacher or counselor, every child needs parents equal to the task of maintaining an orderly, relaxed home. Homes especially adapted to the maximum development of children use a democratic, cooperative family council plan.[4] Begin simply. Call the family together for a talk about a vacation trip or a family picnic—anything pleasant and of interest to all members. Another time issue a call to consider a big problem such as a move to a new neighborhood or a necessary change in family allowances. From these beginnings, it is easy to progress to discussions about the division of labor in the home, about getting-up or going-to-bed routines, or other domestic situations which cause friction. Each family must work out procedures to keep the meetings comfortably short. Perhaps only one subject should be discussed at a get-together, followed by some time for thought, and an alloted time for each family member to explain his suggestion. By a show of hands the most popular solution can then be determined. Majority decisions may be tried for a week or a month. If the situation is not satisfactory, the problem can be discussed again and new solutions negotiated. Families who can work out problems in this way grow in closeness and sensitivity. The children develop a feeling of responsibility for their share of the work and for their part in planning the fun because they understand what "makes the wheels go round," and sense that they too are important to the family.

Since the majority of children come from homes without such training, teachers and counselors will always encounter children in every group with special problems:

1. The handicapped child who has a physical defect which sets him apart from other children and makes him feel inadequate and different.
2. The retiring child, the day dreamer, who never or rarely participates unless coerced, who plays alone, and who is oversensitive. Such a child may be overlooked, especially if the teacher overemphasizes quiet and order.
3. The hyperactive child who seems always at high tension and often in conflict and confusion.
4. The perfectionist child who is exceptionally neat and very attentive to appearances.

5. The anxious, distressed child who is unduly disturbed over mistakes. He, along with the hyperactive child, may frequently be a nail-biter.
6. The show-off who bids for the center of the stage and resorts to tricks to get it.
7. The braggard, often also the bully, who needs to build himself up with big stories and easy victories because his self-esteem is low.
8. The listless child who is slow, tardy, and procrastinating. If a doctor finds no physical cause for these symptoms, play or group therapy may reveal that they are an attention-getting mechanism or a retaliatory device.
9. The child who always has an alibi, who makes excuses and puts the blame on others or on circumstances.
10. The cheat who uses any means to "get by" or to come out ahead. He is fearful that his own powers will not see him through.
11. The obviously fearful child who shuns companions his own age and size and plays with younger, smaller children. He is apt to be overmodest and may blush easily.

These children need special help at an early age, as early as possible. If they are unresponsive to classroom techniques, where subject matter must consume much time, the teacher should interview their parents and enlist their help. Encourage them to seek help for their child and themselves, for if one member of the family has a severe problem, the other members cannot escape involvement in its cause and in its solution.

REFERENCES

1. Adler, A.: *The Individual Psychology of Alfred Adler*. Edited by H. L. and Rowena R. Ansbacher. New York, Basic Books, 1956, pp. 399–404.
2. Adler, A.: *Understanding Human Nature*. New York, Greenberg, 1927, pp. 279–286.
3. Brooks, Mabelle H.: A camp climate for personality growth. *Individ Psychol Bull*, 5:60–62, 1946.
4. Brooks, Mabelle H.: Training the child for self-discipline. *Individ Psychol Bull*, 7:75–86, 1949.
5. Dreikurs, R.: *The Challenge of Parenthood*. New York, Duell, Sloan and Pearce, 1948, pp. 53–94.

28

THE APPLICATION OF DEMOCRATIC PRINCIPLES IN THE CLASSROOM

Vicki Soltz

WHAT GOES ON in our classrooms today is often more tragic than educational. Even though teachers may be well trained in methodology, dedicated to their work, and deeply concerned with the welfare of their students, they are often ill prepared to cope with the disciplinary problems which today's children present.

Many teachers sincerely want to apply democratic techniques, while others are intent upon "showing these kids who is in authority here." In the latter classroom, the students are paying more attention to the game of "who is boss" than to the subject matter; learning is greatly impeded and class discipline becomes paramount. On the other hand, the teacher who wishes to be democratic frequently finds herself facing anarchy in her classroom because she lacks training in effective guidance procedures. It is easy enough to teach the child who wants to learn, but what can the teacher do for the child who obviously does not care or for the child who is determined that no one is going to tell him what to do?

If today's teachers hope to influence children, they need a working knowledge of useful democratic techniques. The inferior child/superior teacher relationship has become obsolete in our democratic social climate. Now we must all learn to function in an atmosphere of equality in interpersonal relationships. Difficulty in understanding the concept of equality lies in the meaning of the word. In math, equal means "the same as," but in human relationships, one person is never "the same as" another. Applied to human relationships, equality means that each

197

individual has the same right as another to decide for himself what he will do—to be self-determining. Equality demands mutual respect: each is obligated to respect his own right to decide for himself and to respect this same right in another, and no one may be permitted to impose his will upon another. We must function without fighting or giving in. Without mutual respect, we violate what Adler called the logic of communal living.[1] When we try to impose our will upon another, we attempt to push him down, and, by implication, elevate ourselves. Much student rebellion is provoked by adult attempts to pressure students into compliance. As a nine-year-old attending voluntary summer school put it, "I just love summer school because here they *let* us learn; the don't *make* us know."

In an often unrecognized but culturally deep-seated prejudice against children, we assume that, since they are small and we are big, we have the right to impose our will upon them. When confronted with principles of mutual respect, many adults panic initially: "If I cannot impose my will upon my children or in the classroom, they will run wild. Children simply can't be allowed to do as they please. I know more than they do and therefore they must learn from me and do as I say. I *have* to be in control." Such thoughts are understandable, but an adult who feels that misbehaving children are out of control merely needs to look closely to discover that the truth is really the reverse: these children are completely *in* control. They know exactly how to make adults, who stand helplessly shouting, do as they wish. Our efforts to control usually prove futile and provoke rebellion.

It is accepted that the obligation of educators is to teach children prescribed subject matter and to "train them for life" as well. How can this be done?

To begin with, the teacher can no longer see herself as an authority, teaching each of twenty-five to thirty pupils, but must become the leader of a group which is an entity in itself. Authority is no longer centered in the individual but in the needs of the total situation—in the demands of reality.[3] In such a climate, learning becomes a group project; the teacher acts as guide who takes the students into partnership to accomplish a given task.

In order to reach these educational goals, the teacher must first understand the individual child and what makes him choose as he does. Next she must be aware of his position in the group. Finally, she must comprehend the total group interaction. Using this information, the teacher can provide meaningful experiences in the classroom. To respect a child's right to be self-determining by no means implies that we allow him to do as he pleases; such permissiveness leads to anarchy. Our duty is to learn methods by which we can *influence the misbehaving child to change his decisions*. Since we cannot impose our decisions upon him, we must guide him into making a new choice. This is the basis for democratic discipline. We provide experiences for the child which stimulate him into changing his mind and, at the same time express confidence that he will move in a constructive direction.

Each child, as he arrives in school, brings with him individual methods for finding his place which have proved successful in his home environment. If he has become discouraged by real or imagined difficulties, he may have based his approach upon faulty or mistaken concepts ("I have a place only if I am first, I have worth only if I can make others do as I wish, I exist if others pay attention to me.") The child's behavior tells the teacher a great deal if she is trained to interpret his movement. The clue to the child's purpose often lies in the teacher's response. Does she frequently ask Mary to stop talking? Does Mary stop for the moment? Mary desires undue attention. Does the teacher feel angry at Mark's disruptive antics? Mark seeks to show his power. Does she feel hurt at Ruth's expressions of contempt? Ruth looks for revenge. Is Beth absolutely hopeless? Beth wants to be let alone and is completely discouraged; she fears that any attempt on her part will reveal and make more humiliating her assumed uselessness.

Knowledge of the child's interpretation of his position within his family (family constellation), his physical handicaps (if present), and family and community values and attitudes are essential for the effective teacher and provide insight into the hidden intentions of the child and his directions of movement.

Today's children are far more influenced by their relationship with their classmates than they are by their relationship to the teacher. While some children may work best when they establish a "special place" with the teacher, their classmates often reject them with the tag, "teacher's pet." Such alliances disrupt the group, producing factions which prevent group integration. Unless the teacher develops skills in uniting the group as a whole, she is helpless in the face of the opposition promoted by subgroups who are against her. Today's children are amazingly united in their determination to defeat the pressure-applying autocratic adult.

Sociometric chains may help to cope with these problems. Even in the first grade a sociogram can be developed to show vividly which children are leaders, which are followers, and which are isolates. A sociogram may demonstrate what the alert teacher suspects but may also provide surprises. It further provides a means whereby the teacher can group the children for project work so that there is a flow of communication from isolate to student leader. Detrimental subgroups can be broken, and the strength of the class as a whole can be utilized for the task at hand.[5]

Having established herself as a leader in partnership, integrated the group into a close-knit working unit and familiarized herself with each child as an individual within the group, the teacher is now prepared to apply specific democratic principles. Of these, encouragement is of paramount importance.

Tragically, many of our teaching devices are actually discouraging to the child! At the top of the list is the practice of competition which damages more children than it stimulates. For every child who seems to progress under the stimulus of "winning," hundreds give up, feeling discouraged and defeated because they sense they are nothing unless they are on top. The child who seems to respond to competition does so because he feels driven to be first, to be on top. His position is perilous, since someone may dislodge him at any time. Should he meet a situation later—as many do in college, for example—where he is no longer "first in his class," his confidence in his own ability and his faith in life are undermined severely and he may break down entirely and be unable to function. Competition further stimulates over-ambition—the feeling that only if one accomplishes great things or huge amounts is one good enough. Having established impossible goals for himself, a youngster's discouragement is reinforced through competition which may serve to prove that he is not good enough. Finally, competition fosters the fictive goal that one has a place and value only when he is superior to others. Such a concept is contrary to the ideals of a democratic society in which all have value by the fact of their existence and in which the obligation of life is to respond to the needs of the total situation. It is difficult for many to believe that children who do not pursue fictive goals can progress and learn for the pure joy of learning, that a sense of achievement comes, not by being measured against what the other fellow does, but from a growing awareness of one's own inner strength and one's capacity to cope with life.

The teacher must avoid discouraging practices but also understand how to encourage children. Cardinal factors in encouragement are faith, acceptance, and the practice of building on strengths. She must have faith in the child's abilities, in his courage and in his desire to achieve— not through competition but through contributing and through a growing awareness of his own strengths. She must also *accept the child as he is now*—not as she expects him to be later. "As you are right now, you are fine. Now let us learn and grow together."

The teacher who encourages is the one who builds on strengths rather than attempting to eliminate weakness. If the child's attention is fastened upon what he must avoid, he has little energy left to apply to growth. "How well you make your *a*'s," is encouragement. The child may be stimulated to feel, "If I can make good *a*'s, I can make good *b*'s too." "Try to make better *b*'s," is discouraging. To say, "You can do better if you try," discourages, since the child hears, "You don't do well enough now." He soon feels, "Oh, what's the use? I can't do it right anyhow."

Praise, which is in effect a reward, shows disrespect and is thereby discouraging. It may be difficult for the teacher to distinguish between praise as recognition and praise as reward, but in all interactions with children, she must separate the deed from the doer. Praise gives false value to the doer, intimating that the doer has worth only if he gains praise. Recognition, on the other hand, acknowledges the deed, the accomplishment, the contribution. "We appreciate the clean blackboard, John." "How tidy your desk looks, Jan." "Your paper is very neat today, Bobby." "That was a well-presented report, Bill. We have learned something." Such comments accept the deed and build on strength. The teacher's obligation is to show the child that he can make a mistake without loss of personal value.

In addition to practicing the art of encouragement, the teacher needs specific methods for coping with misbehavior. One of the most suitable is the idea of putting all the children in the same boat. Since the class must function as a group, it should be treated as a unit. A child may cause a disturbance to keep teacher busy with him. His action loses its value to him, if the class as whole gets what he was after. The effective teacher may quietly say, "We cannot continue until the class is ready." There is tremendous power in quietness.

Punishment is futile as a training device and merely provokes rebellion. Children refuse to be treated as inferiors and to be judged and punished by a "superior." Only a superior being could have the prerogative to decide who is worthy of reward and who deserves punishment. In a classroom of equals, there can be no superior being condescending to reward or presuming to punish. The teacher who resorts to punishment declares her inadequacy in coping with behavior problems.

The principle of natural and logical consequences can be adapted to the classroom. A natural consequence can be defined as what follows a violation of order if no adult interferes. However, in some instances, it may be unwise to wait: Bobby cannot be allowed to throw stones on the playground until someone gets a bloody head. Since there can be no freedom without order, one loses his freedom when he violates order. In such cases, logical consequences can be structured to meet the situation. Since Bobby's behavior violates safety and order, he must leave—for the present. Encouragement is vital at this point. "We feel sure you will learn quickly how to behave. You may try again at the next recess."

Respect for a child's decision to misbehave may be clearly shown. He is given to understand that he is sent out of the room not *because* he misbehaves but *for as long as he chooses to misbehave.* "Mark, you apparently don't feel like joining us. You may leave the room until you feel like behaving."

Logical consequences can become retaliatory and if punishing, the teacher feels angry. The effective teacher, therefore, looks not at the threat to her personal "control" over the student and the classroom but at the needs of the total situation and then moves to restore order.[2]

While kindness and friendliness are essential, so also is firmness. The art lies in being firm without dominating. The teacher must decide what *she* will do, not what she will *make the student do.* "I will not tolerate talking aloud in my classroom" may seem to be a statement of teacher action, but actually means, "I will make you keep quiet." "I will not talk when you do," on the other hand, reinforces the teacher's decision and places group pressure on the talkers, thus avoiding a power contest between teacher and student.

In coping with misbehavior, avoid acting on impulse. If the classroom is noisy, the first impulse may be to talk louder in order to be heard. If the teacher does the unexpected and lowers her voice, the children respond accordingly.

Sidestep a struggle for power in managing classroom behavior. If a child wants to show that no one can boss him, he may insist on standing when the class is sitting. "If you decide to stand, there is nothing I can do about it. But I would appreciate it very much if you would sit down." With this statement, the teacher recognizes the child's power to decide. She cannot stop the child from acting as he is, but she can make it ineffective for him to continue. Her second statement may encourage the child to cooperate. Teacher resentment toward the student who seems to "get by with something" is due to the mistaken idea that she must *control* him rather than *train* him.

Just as families may profit from conducting a weekly family council, so also can a class benefit from regularly scheduled group discussions. In this situation, the teacher needs the skill to *listen* and to ask the right questions. She must have an inner freedom which permits her to accept differences of opinion without feeling a challenge to her personal prestige. Group discussion implies the coordinated effort of all in seeking solutions to problems. It precludes preaching, moralizing, or the imposition of personal values by the teacher. As a leader of group discussion, she must guide the discussion away from anarchy and random expression of opinion into meaningful channels. As children begin to understand each other, they also develop a desire to help each other. Individual students find a sense of participation and contribution, and the class becomes closely integrated.

Anything from procedure for a class project to personal problems may be discussed at these sessions. If a child complains of a classmate cheating, the teacher can suggest that this subject be discussed at the weekly session. The class needs no sermon about the wrongness of cheating, and the teacher may be astonished to discover at what an early age children know right from wrong. Because they sometimes fail to act on this knowledge is merely part of their hidden, mistaken goals. A productive discussion may center around questions such as the following: "For what purpose does one cheat? What are the advantages? What are the disadvantages?" When one child expresses an opinion the teacher asks others what they think about that idea. Through carefully questioning, by interrupting sermons, and by interjecting phrases such as, "How does this help us to be friends?", the teacher guides the children toward mutual understanding.

Group discussion has many pitfalls and should be undertaken only after study of the procedure.[4] However, if the teacher aids the class in considering "purposes" or "gains" rather than "causes," she refrains from preaching and induces the pupils to express their ideas, and if she encourages class examination of these ideas, she is functioning as a discussion leader. The teacher who uses democratic principles to guide her students experiences a sense of personal achievement, successfully meets the needs of the total classroom situation, and satisfactorily fulfills the requirements of her profession.

REFERENCES

1. Adler, A.: *Social Interest: A Challenge To Mankind.* New York, Capricorn Books, 1964, pp. 269–285.
2. Dreikurs, R., and Grey, L.: *Logical Consequences.* New York, Meredith Press, 1968, pp. 62–82.
3. Dreikurs, R., and Soltz, V.: *Children: The Challenge.* New York, Duell, Sloan & Pearce, 1964, pp. 152–153.
4. Grunwald, B.: The Application of Adlerian Principles in the Classroom. Published by the Oregon Society of Individual Psychology, 1954.
5. Jennings, H. H.: *Sociometry in Group Relations.* Washington, D.C., American Council on Education, 1959.

29

JOINT COUNSELING WITH PARENTS AND TEENS

Genevieve Painter

ADLER [1] maintained that an essential function of the school is to prepare students to meet the tasks of life outside the academic institution and to become useful to society. According to him, the primary objective of education is to prepare the student for social living and for proper relationships with his fellow man. He applied democratic principles in pedagogy by stressing openness and cooperation between parents and students and advocated sessions between them to lessen the distance that frequently exists between parents and offspring. Adolescents often search for values, question the behavior of adults, harbor doubts about school and society, and wish to achieve a sense of meaning and purpose for themselves. Adler's notion of pedagogy is addressed to this adolescent quest.

Dreikurs [3] developed these ideas of proposing "truce meetings" between parents and children or adolescents at which each member learned how the others thought. He wanted to demonstrate that children and adolescents should participate in the decisions which affect them. When young people feel they have a *place* in society and *share* in decisions which concern the welfare of everyone, they are less likely to fight the "system" or to reject their parents.[2] The counseling procedure discussed in this paper adopts an Adlerian perspective and may be implemented by sophisticated teachers in the primary and secondary classroom or by parents and their adolescent children at home.

"It is not only that parents are no longer guides, but that there are no guides," writes Margaret Mead in her new book, *Culture and Commitment*.[5] The family counselor can provide ample documentation of that statement, for there no longer seem to be sets of values—absolutes of right or wrong—in which parents definitely believe. The mother raised by a strict sexual code discovers that her beliefs are now considered old fashioned and begins to question their validity. She finds herself in conflict between personal adherence to older mores and her more flexible attitude toward newer ones. When dealing with her teenage daughter, she may preach the older mores but doubt the soundness of her sermons. Frequently parents themselves disagree; one may be more conservative in his beliefs than the other and neither is completely sure he is right. Such self-doubts may result in each parent blaming the other for the problems with the children.

As the conflict between parent and child grows, the peer group increasingly becomes the dominant model of behavior for the teenager. The generation gap widens. The rebellion of young people against "the establishment" cuts across social, racial, and economic lines and has, in fact, become worldwide in scope.

In an attempt to help parents who are in conflict with their "normal" teenagers, the author established family group counseling sessions. Parents complained of their youngsters' lack of respect for parental authority or their open defiance. Their children, they felt, wanted their own way at all times, were away from the home too frequently and too late at night, conducted longlasting and frequent telephone calls, spent too little time on homework, improperly selected their friends, wore their hair too long regardless of sex, and refused to carry out assigned household chores. In general, the parents were suspicious about what the youngsters might be up to. The teens, on the other hand, complained that parents were unreasonable and unfair, refused to listen or to try to understand, did not trust them, and did not tell them the true reasons for their worry and restrictions. In general, the youngsters considered their parents nosey.

Four sets of parents who were having problems with their fifteen- to sixteen-year-old children consulted the author. Each family was seen at first as an individual family unit. *All* members of each family, even those children with whom the parents did not believe that they had problems, were included. At the initial session each family member was asked what he would like to see improved in his family. As the session progressed, one problem area was chosen by the counselor for emphasis, and suggestions for solutions were given by each family member. Agreement was not, of course, reached, but the counselor clarified some of the interactions among the family members and some of the underlying purposes of their conflicts.

The family was encouraged to conduct a weekly family council where each member would be allowed to say what he thought about the family's problems. As a group they would see what they might do to get along better. The only direction given by the counselor was that the meeting be stopped if there were fights. Family members were merely to practice listening to each other and were not to come to conclusions or to make decisions. Only later, after they could listen to each other without anger, should they try to come to agreement.

The children in these families (three fifteen-year-old girls and one sixteen-year-old boy) formed the nucleus of a separate teenage counseling group. They invited friends to join the group which met weekly and included six to nine youngsters. Once a month their parents were invited to attend these sessions. The group has been kept open to newcomers and at this writing has met for four months. One girl from the original group dropped out, but her parents have continued to attend the monthly sessions. Parents were also encouraged to enter community reading-discussion groups which focused their study on *Children: The Challenge* by Dreikurs and Soltz.[4]

The teens choose their own topics for discussion each week, guided by one counselor-initiated question at the beginning of each session: "Is anything in particular bothering you today?" Usually one or more of the group has a complaint, perhaps something as commonplace as how her mother has been nagging her to clean up her room. That problem may reveal similar ones among the group and the discussion is begun. The counselor allows the discussion to flow freely but interprets the underlying purposes of behavior within the family, such as an unwillingness to accept responsibility or a demonstration of power against someone who attempts to *make* us do a chore.

One day these teens talked of how their religious beliefs differed from those of their parents. Each concluded from his earlier experiences that Sunday school existed merely to keep children amused and not as a place for learning about religion, values, or ethics, as their parents seemed to believe. Coloring pictures of Jesus Christ, one recalled, was the main activity of the church school; another thought that activity was better than the pictures of ships he drew in class. While parents must obviously have viewed these classes as religious training for their children, the children themselves understood there had to be more to religion. As one girl said, "I know that God is with me if I walk alone at night." Another commented, "I am not sure if there is a God, but I would not dare say that to my parents."

The initial embarrassment at "bringing out the family wash" was banished as children and parents realized their problems were not unique. One fifteen-year-old was distressed because her parents placed what she called an "unreasonable" time limit on her telephone calls and felt that this issue caused the most serious trouble between them. During the teen session the following week, which was attended by parents, this girl watched silently as various parents and children disagreed openly on a variety of issues. At the conclusion of the session she commented, "When I saw the problems other kids had with their parents, mine didn't seem so bad after all." Her damaged relationship with her parents began to improve after this insight. She was not quite as hostile to her parents and they began to become more accepting of her.

From youthful dress to the kind of friends parents approve of—the discussions continue but not merely as endless talk. The underlying goals of behavior are interpreted and conflicts between teens and parents are explored; ideas on how to solve these problems are exchanged. This kind of exchange—between a child and his or the parents of others, between parents and their own children or the children of others —is often a surprising relief to discouraged teens and parents and the beginning of new and meaningful communication. As the teens and parents become more understanding of their interactions, the gap between the generations is reduced and the possibility for actions which may resolve or lessen family conflict is restored.

REFERENCES

1. Adler, A.: *Superiority and Social Interest.* Edited by H. L. and Rowena R. Ansbacher. Evanston, Ill., Northwestern University Press, 1964, pp. 304–307.
2. Dinkmeyer, D., and Dreikurs, R.: *Encouraging Children to Learn.* Englewood Cliffs: Prentice-Hall, 1963, pp. 122–123.

3. Dreikurs, R.: Can We Find Peace Between the Generations? In W. L. Pew (Ed.): *The War Between The Generations*. Minneapolis, Minnesota Society of Individual Psychology, 1968, pp. 33–43.
4. Dreikurs, R., and Soltz, V.: *Children: The Challenge*. Duell, Sloan and Pearce, 1968.
5. Mead, M.: *Culture and Commitment*. New York, Doubleday, 1970.

30

MENTAL HEALTH PROPHYLAXIS

Paul Brodsky

MENTAL HEALTH is the manifestation of the individual's integration into society. For this reason, various levels of mental health can reflect the degree of integration into society and may correspond to the developmental levels of the individual as he grows from infancy toward adulthood. Thus, a lack of recognition of one's self as part of a whole (integration) might be considered normal or mentally healthy in a neonate, a symptom of serious mental disorder in an adolescent, and a symptom of even more serious disorder in an adult.

At this point, it may prove helpful to differentiate between integrating and conforming, since both responses express a recognition of the existing social environment and rely on cooperation to some extent. The integrated person may offer cooperation through his originality, individuality, creativeness and opposition, but he may also conform when he recognizes the need for such behavior, as, for example, conforming to the arrangements necessary to assist a person in distress, conforming to team rules, conforming in deference to the rituals of a religious ceremony to which he has been invited. Since his actions are the result of a conscious decision, he will accept the responsibility for their consequences. In contrast, the conformist may adopt his attitude in order to satisfy his vanity, to gain recognition as "a good sport," to rate as "the guy you can always depend upon," or to be "the trusted, loyal citizen." In contrast to integration, conformity promises relief from the responsibility for decision and consequent actions, although that relief may be merely temporary. Since the conformist is inclined to do what he is supposed to do, what everybody does, what *they* want him to do, he will, obviously, express little originality and creativeness. Because conformity demands submission, the conformist may harbor feelings of rebellion against the source of these demands and feel obligated, guilty, resentful, and hostile. Often these feelings are then directed toward society at large.

One measure of mental health is the relationship between the individual's level of integration and his developmental level, particularly the extent to which he has shifted from infantile dependency toward the interdependency of adulthood.[1] It is well to keep in mind that the opposite of dependency is not independency, for the search for independency as an experience of self is merely a phase characteristic of adolescence. Successfully breaking through childhood dependency, however, to seek independent identity is prerequisite to integration. While dependency is mentally healthy for the infant, the search for independence is mentally healthy for the adolescent, and the achievement of interdependency is mentally healthy for the adult. The degree of success in achieving these developmental steps toward integration is symptomatic of the individual's level of mental health. During the process of integration, the dominance of basic needs shifts from those of infancy to the higher needs of the maturing individual who evolves from the position of a recipient of love (childhood), finds himself a part of a whole, and, as an adult, becomes a source of love and care for others.

Mental health is reflected in still another way: the interrelatedness of the individual, beyond his fellow man, to art, nature, and universe. Man's relentlessly questioning mind, first shown in childhood curiosity, is his main support in his bid for security and survival and brings him face to face with nature and the vastness of the universe. In order to find a place in the universe, man strives to encompass it imaginatively. Through expressing these thoughts and feelings, he establishes a relationship with that extra-human environment. Beyond the relatively small wholeness of human society, the "I-you" relations, he finds himself included in the cosmic wholeness of the universe; and his inquiries of "where from," "where to," and "what for" provide greater meaning for his life.

To expand beyond one's self, to merge into the needs of someone or something outside of the self, is to *love*. The individual's capability for loving is, consequently, another indication of his level of mental health.

To love, apparently, presupposes freedom from dependency o1
object.[2] Unless one has found one's own self, one cannot expa
it, and that is why children, in the process of finding thei
cannot be expected to love. That is also why love is incompatible with
poor mental health which is always accompanied by self-centeredness.

It is important to recognize the mind as the factor in the living
organism which coordinates external and internal stimuli toward the
general goal of survival. The mind, in fact, is the "self" experienced by
the individual in his identity. In striving for personal identity, he joins
in the identity of man as species and in the task of its self-preservation
according to the laws of nature. His contribution toward the common
survival goal of the species is discerned in his usefulness, in his actions
which benefit others.

Mental health prophylaxis and the definition of mental health put
forth in this paper suggest that children must be provided with an
environment in which they may grow without the danger that everyday
educational situations can become trigger situations for emotional disorder. The prevention of mental disturbance, as in all prophylactic orientations, focuses on the "well child" instead of the emotionally endangered one and emphasizes those aspects of environment which have the
greatest potential for control—the home and early school surroundings.
Workers in the area of the mental health of children must recognize
that the child's mind often comes to erroneous conclusions and abstractions because it interprets stimuli in limited experience and with limited
comprehension; upon the erroneous abstractions of childhood, the individual may form a ficticious life concept. To discover these misconceptions and to assist in their correction is the foremost task of education at
home as well as at school.[4]

It is well to differentiate between primary and secondary prevention,
since some grade-school children have already developed behavior patterns which require professional treatment but which cannot be considered neurotic. Primary prevention is directed toward handling normal
educational situations skillfully in order to arrive at acceptable solutions;
secondary prevention concerns the handling of situations which
threaten to become more serious problems and to avert such deteriora-
tion. Primary prevention is concerned with the educational problems of
children during the formative and grade school years; secondary prevention deals with preteens and adolescents in secondary school. The

family, which functions as the first educational unit, demands the interest of a preventive approach. This approach is also important in the elementary school which handles the child while he is still closely connected with his home surroundings. It is imperative that the findings of modern pedagogy and psychology be made available to both of these educational units so that they can prepare the child to meet the demands of the society as a whole. A preventive approach to problems of mental health must help parents, teachers, and mental health workers to adjust themselves and their educational concepts to the general evolution of society, to come to realize that love and dedication alone are not sufficient to teach children what they need to know to face the challenges of a rapidly changing world.

A preventive approach to mental health problems must concern itself with the early detection of emotional disturbance and with the prevention of conditions conducive to the development of such disturbances. Such an approach is based on the assumption that most parents love their children and act in their best interests so far as parental understanding and experiences permit. In order to safeguard the parental ego, a preventive approach must center on the improvement of child-rearing skills as a supplement to love and dedication. To that end, a differentiation between knowing and understanding a child is helpful: Parents know their children, that is, from experience they have learned to anticipate a child's response to a given situation. Mother knows what makes Susie break out with hives; that Jimmy's answer to "What homework have you got?" will always be "None."; that every attempt at coaching Bob with his spelling words will end with her frustration and anger and with Bob in tears but happy that the session is over for today. The teacher knows that Helen always drops things during class, that Tim never has an answer to a direct question but will pipe up as soon as another child has been called upon, that Evelyn makes her nervous by moving about noiselessly and keeping herself constantly at teacher's side. Understanding a child, however, means to see his actions and behavior as manifestations of motivations toward goals. An individual's behavior is meaningful and purposeful regardless of whether the individual is aware of his goal, and a child's response to particular situations in his life (school, siblings, home surroundings) will reflect his interpretation of these situations. Susan's hives reflect her body chemistry, but her reason for continuing to eat strawberries reflect her motivation—perhaps her desire to be like everyone else, or to be liked by her hostess who served strawberries for her birthday party, or to prove to her mother that she could not regulate Susan's life. Jim may answer that he has no homework to avoid being tied down all afternoon but may also reflect his discouragement with mathematics or his fear to face the English class with a book report. Evelyn may move silently so that the teacher will not send her back to her seat, but her noiseless hovering may also indicate her fear of being ugly or clumsy and unwanted by her classmates whom she hopes to outdistance by being teacher's pet.

Parents and teachers usually respond to a child's actions rather than to his motivations; yet, his behavior reflects his interpretation of a situation, and is the manifestation of his motivations. His misbehavior may stem from his own misinterpretations and misunderstandings; however, misinterpretations and misunderstandings are also made by his parents, his teachers, and others close to him. The combination of parental familiarity with the child and the observations by trained staff members at school should aid in the early identification of childhood difficulties and in the initiation of preventive measures.[3] The close cooperation of home and school is indispensable in a preventive approach, and opportunities for such cooperation should be provided by the public school system. Such liaison would, in addition, avert parents' concern over the stigma associated with seeking professional help from private and semiprivate agencies.

School mental health services can be instituted within a limited financial outlay and within a framework similar to that of remedial reading classes or special classes for the hard of hearing. Families will need to be screened, so that children and parents with acute emotional problems will be referred for some other form of guidance or therapy. The screening should be based upon a physician's report, a school report, tests and observations—many of which may be available in school records. Because special facilities are not needed, unoccupied classrooms may be utilized for this program which would be under the supervision of the health and guidance departments of the school system. By aligning parent-education classes of the Parent-Teacher Association and the Adult Education Programs of the school districts with such a program of prevention, wide public interest and support can be promoted. Close cooperation between home and school also facilitates follow-up studies to determine the length of counseling necessary in a given case. It is of importance to keep in mind, however, that a preventive approach is not limited to a particular school child but serves as a general assistance to parents and teachers in adjusting their educational skills and their concepts to the demands of a changing society. The preventive services offered must be available at any time to help a family with a specific educational problem at home or at school or to allow them to improve their knowledge and skills by using the service as a more general learning situation.

Finally, a preventive approach to problems of mental health can help to alleviate the manpower shortage within the area of public mental health. Since a preventive approach is primarily an educational approach, school psychologists, social workers, and school administrators could be trained to implement it, and a new source of professional manpower would be tapped. Psychiatrists and clinical psychologists could then be freed to serve those in need of highly skilled professional help. There is little doubt that an increase of services to implement a preventive approach would do much to combat the number two threat to public health—mental health disorders.

REFERENCES

1. Adler, A.: *The Individual Psychology of Alfred Adler*. Edited by H. L. and Rowena R. Ansbacher, New York, Basic Books, 1956, pp. 101–125.
2. Brodsky, P.: Dependence-interdependence. *The Individual Psychologist*, 1, No. 2, 1963.
3. Brodsky, P.: Problems of adolescence: An Adlerian view. *Adolescence*, 3:9–22, 1968.
4. Dreikurs, R.: *Fundamentals of Adlerian Psychology*. Chicago, Alfred Adler Institute, 1950, pp. 73–84.

EPILOGUE

The value of this book depends on the benefit which the reader may derive from it. There can be no doubt that he will gain new insights into human problems and their solutions. But the book is more than a practical guide; it reflects a philosophy of social living so desperately needed in this era of transition. What gives this book its special significance is its concise presentation of the model of man which Adler proposed.

Adler was fifty years ahead of his time, and his basic ideas clashed with those of his contemporaries. There was little recognition that man was a decision-making organism, that he had the ability to choose and to decide. Such an assumption ran counter to scientific promulgation and prompted Adler to train lay people to use his techniques in teaching, in guidance, and in therapy—a practice which widened the gap between him and the professional community. Social and behavioral scientists considered man the victim of forces which converged on him from within and without, but Adler envisioned a new concept of man as master of his fate.

Two fundamentally new findings made in this century are bound to affect greatly the future of mankind. One is the discovery of the tremendous and totally unexpected power within the atom; the other is the realization of the tremendous power and strength within each individual. Man had been considered small in time and space, like a grain of sand on the beach, coming from dust and becoming dust. Now we begin to realize the potential strength within each individual, a capacity which at present is only minimally used. Adler showed us how to release these immense energies, a means of freeing man from his deep inferiority feelings, of preventing discouragement and of evoking social interest, which is the basis for normal functioning.

Adler recognized a logic of social living and stands in stark contrast to those who are pessimistic about man's ability to live at peace with his fellowmen. He pointed to the crucial deficiency of our time—our inability to perceive the equality we have reached in a democratic society and our lack of a tradition by which we may live with each other as equals. For him, equality was the basis for social harmony, for the recognition of the "Ironclad Logic of Social Living."

His concrete suggestions for education, guidance, and psychotherapy are based on the necessity to get along with one's fellowman on the basis of mutual respect. Although he was opposed and ignored by those who did not understand him, we witness now his great success. It is tragic, and encouraging, that at the centennial of his birth he is held in higher repute than during his lifetime.

As we read his books, we are forced to recognize that the demands he made for better homes, better schools, and a better society are today as unfulfilled as they were fifty years ago. Yet, the correctness of his thesis becomes increasingly obvious to a constantly widening circle of professionals and lay people. While other schools of thought have had to change and readjust the basic tenets of their teachers, Adler's model of man survived intact and needs no revision. What greater proof can one have of its validity?

We who followed his example have the satisfaction of seeing society move in the direction which he visualized. The reason for the amazing revival of Individual Psychology is simple: Adler's concept of man is needed in a democratic society. Personality theories always express the cultural climate. In an autocratic society, one had to believe in the force of heredity and hold that personality is determined in the moment of conception. As our society became more democratic, the emphasis shifted to environmental influences. Society was held responsible for inadequate development or deviation. Freud's influence has been attributed to his shattering of the Victorian sexual mores. Actually, these mores did not exist in Vienna, and the Viennese did not need Freud to free them sexually. One can attribute Freud's success to the fact that he expressed the demands of rugged individualism, that he spoke for the rights and needs of the individual against a repressive society.

It was Adler's genius to oppose all such explanations of man's behavior. He recognized man as a free agent who was able to decide for himself. It is this belief in man's capacity to change which gives Adlerians their proverbial optimism. We know that everyone *can* change, although we cannot know whether he *will* change. Adler conveyed his deep trust in man to his students. He stated that every criminal can be rehabilitated if his confidence is won; he declared categorically that no child is hopeless.

The reader of this book must keep in mind the need to alter our mechanistic and pessimistic view of man. One cannot accept the technical procedures which Adler proposed without accepting his philosophy, his model of man.

RUDOLF DREIKURS, M.D.

INDEX